THE CENTRAL CONCEPTION OF BUDDHISM

AND

THE MEANING OF THE WORD "DHARMA"

THE CENTRAL CONCEPTION OF BUDDHISM AND THE MEANING OF THE WORD "DHARMA"

BY

TH. STCHERBATSKY, PH.D.,

PROFESSOR IN THE UNIVERSITY OF PETROGRAD, MEMBER OF THE ACADEMY OF SCIENCES OF RUSSIA

MOTILAL BANARSIDASS
DELHI :: PATNA :: VARANASI

©MOTILAL BANARSIDASS
Indological Publishers & Booksellers
Head Office : BUNGALOW ROAD, JAWAHARNAGAR, DELHI-7
Branches : 1. CHOWK, VARANASI-1 (U. P.)
2. ASHOK RAJPATH, PATNA-4 (BIHAR)

adhidharma

First Edition published by Royal Asiatic Society, London : 1923
Reprinted by M/s. Motilal Banarsidass, Delhi : 1970, 1974

Price : Rs. 12.00

Printed in India
BY SHANTILAL JAIN, AT SHRI JAINENDRA PRESS, BUNGALOW ROAD, JAWAHARNAGAR, DELHI-7 AND PUBLISHED BY SUNDARLAL JAIN FOR MOTILAL BANARSIDASS, BUNGALOW ROAD, JAWAHARNAGAR, DELHI-7

CONTENTS

PREFACE

THIS short treatise was originally conceived as a contribution to the Royal Asiatic Society's *Journal*: its size induced the Council to publish it as a monograph, and my best thanks are due to the Council for this kind decision. I must also express my gratitude to Mrs. C. A. F. Rhys Davids, who was always ready to help with her vast knowledge of Pali literature. Professor H. Jacobi kindly went through the proofs, and to him I am indebted for many a valuable suggestion. Dr. McGovern contributed some of the references to Chinese sources. But my deepest gratitude is due to Dr. F. W. Thomas, who devoted much of his precious time to the revision of my work and to carrying it through the press.

In transliteration I have usually not distinguished the guttural, etc., nasals, when occurring before the consonants of their respective classes.

TH. STCHERBATSKY.

July, 1923.

The central conception of Buddhism and the meaning of the term *Dharma*

I. Preliminary

IN a recent work Mrs. M. Geiger and Professor W. Geiger have made an attempt to solve the uncertainty which still prevails about the meaning of the term *dharma*.[1] They have drawn up a concordance of almost every case where the word occurs in Pali canonical literature, and established a great variety of meanings. Among them there is, indeed, only one that really matters, that is the specifically Buddhistic technical term *dharma*. The other significations which Buddhist literature shares with the Brahmanical do not present any serious difficulty. About this meaning the authors rightly remark that it is a " central conception of the Buddhist doctrine which must be elucidated as far as possible ". They also contend that the method followed by them is " purely philological ". This is also an indication of the limitations of their work, because the central conception of a highly complicated system, a conception which in its varied connotations includes almost the totality of the system, cannot be expected to be fully elucidated by " philological " methods only. We therefore propose, in addition to Mrs. and Professor Geiger's most valuable collections, to consider the matter from the philosophical standpoint, i.e. to give, with regard to this conception, a succinct account of the system in which it admittedly occupies the keystone position. Our chief source will be, not the Pali Canon, but a later work, the *Abhidharma-koça* of Vasubandhu.[2] Although late, it is professedly

[1] *Pali Dhamma*, von Magdalene u. Wilhelm Geiger, Munich, 1921.

[2] A plan of an edition and translation of the whole work has been outlined and partly carried through by the *Bibliotheca Buddhica* at Petrograd. There have appeared, (1) *Abhidharma-koça-kārikā* and *Bhāṣya*, Tibetan

only a systematized exposition of a much earlier work—the *Abhidharma-vibhāṣā-çāstra*, which, in its turn, is but a commentary on the *abhidharma* of the Sarvāstivādin school. This school is one of the earliest, if not the earliest, of Buddhist sects. The question upon which it dissented and from which it received its name had a bearing on the essence of what was called a *dharma*, so that an exposition of its views will afford the best opportunity of examining the full connotation of this term.[1] It must be left to later investigation to determine the points where Vasubandhu's exposition may be at variance with the primitive doctrine; but, generally speaking, he seems to have rendered the original doctrine very faithfully. Since his age is about the same as that of the Pali commentaries,[2] the difference between him and the

text, pt. i, edited by Professor Th. Stcherbatsky, Petrograd, 1917; (2) *Sphuṭārthābhidharma-koça-vyākhyā* of Yaçomitra, Sanscrit text, pt. i, edited by S. Lévi and Th. Stcherbatsky, Petrograd, 1917. The second parts of both these works, Tibetan text edition by Professor Th. Stcherbatsky and Vyākhyā (Sanscrit) by Professor W. Wogihara of Tokyo, are being printed in the *Bibliotheca Buddhica*. An English translation of the ninth (additional) part has been published by Professor Th. Stcherbatsky under the title "The Soul Theory of the Buddhists" in the *Bulletin de l'Académie des Sciences de Russie*, Petrograd, 1920 (pp. 823–54 and 937–58). A review of the system has been published by the late Professor O. Rosenberg, of Petrograd University, under the title *Problems of Buddhist Philosophy*, Petrograd, 1918 (in Russian). This scholar has also issued an index of Buddhist technical terms in Chinese and Japanese under the title *An Introduction to the study of Buddhism from Chinese and Japanese Sources*, Tokyo, 1917. Professor de la Vallée Poussin has published in Brussels a French translation of the third part, and is now engaged in printing a translation of the first and second parts of the *Abhidharma-koça*.

1 Beside Mrs. and Prof. Geiger the question has been treated by Mrs. Rhys Davids, *Bud. Psy. Ethics*, xxxiii; Walleser, *Grundlage*, 97–104; Warren, *Buddhism in Translations*, 116, 209; S. Z. Aung, *Compendium*, 179 n., 254–9; S. Lévi, *Sūtrālaṃkāra*, 18, 21; L. de la Vallée Poussin, *Notes sur les corps du Bouddha*, Muséon, 1913, pp. 263, 287. The question has been put in the proper light and brilliantly treated by Professor O. Rosenberg, *Problems*, chap. vi: but, since his work is written in Russian and inaccessible at present, some of his results are repeated here.

2 The date of Vasubandhu is not yet quite settled; cf. the references in V. Smith, *Early History*, 3rd ed., pp. 328 ff. At the end of chap. viii Vasubandhu remarks that in his time the *āgama* had had an existence of

Pali sources is not so much one of time as of school. Nothing is more instructive than the study of the divergent views of different schools, since it allows us to watch the builders of the Buddhist doctrine at work.

The formula of the Buddhist Credo (*ye dhammā*, etc.)—which professedly contains the shortest statement of the essence and the spirit of Buddhism [1]—declares that Buddha discovered the elements (*dhammā*) of existence, their causal connexion, and a method to suppress their efficiency for ever (*nirodho*). Vasubandhu makes a similar statement about the essence of the doctrine: it is a method of converting the elements of existence into a condition of rest, out of which they never will emerge again.[2] From the first days of the Buddhist church the novices, before obtaining admittance into the order, went through a course of instruction in what may be termed the Buddhist catechism, i.e. an exposition of the elements (*dharma*) of existence and their different classifications into *skandhas, āyatanas, dhātus*.[3] The same training was considered indispensable for the aspiring nuns.[4] These conditions have not changed down to the present day in all Buddhist countries. In the whole of Mongolia and Tibet, in those parts of Siberia where Buddhism is spreading against the primitive Shamanism among the Tunguz tribes of

1,000 (not 900) years, and the *adhigama* (=*abhidharma*) somewhat less than that. That there were two Vasubandhus is not "a guess with no solid basis"; the Koça actually quotes the opinions of a *vṛiddhācārya* Vasubandhu and rejects them (i, 13, Tibetan text, p. 23; cf. Yaçomitra's comment) There remain the dates of the Chinese translations of the works of Asanga and Vasubandhu, which alone, if correct, would be sufficient evidence to assign them to the fourth century. Otherwise one feels inclined to bring Vasubandhu nearer to Dignāga, whose teacher he was.

[1] Cf. *Mahāvagga*, i, 23.

[2] *Ab. K.*, i, 1, Tib. text, p. 3, ll. 12–15.

[3] Cf. *Theragāthā*, 1255:

tassāhaṃ vacanaṃ sutvā khandhe āyatanāni ca
dhātuyo ca viditvāna pabbajiṃ anāgariyaṃ.

[4] Cf. Geiger's references to *Therīgāthās*, op. cit., p. 65; the *dhātus* there mentioned are probably the eighteen *dhātus* (not the six); a number of other divisions into *dhātus* are mentioned in the *Bahu-dhātuka-sūtra*, cf. *Ab. K.*, i, 27, Tib. text, p. 46.

Transbaikalia, in the governments of Irkutsk and Astrachan, where it is maintaining itself against orthodox Christianity—everywhere it invariably proceeds by starting religious schools (*chos-grva*), where manuals similar to the *Dhamma-saṃgaṇi* containing tables of *dharmas* are carefully studied, in the Tibetan original with explanations in vernacular, by the young generation aspiring to be admitted to the order and to be gradually promoted to the higher ecclesiastical ranks. Scholars of Buddhism in Europe will do well to follow this example.

A school of Buddhists which claims as its fundamental doctrine the principle that "everything exists" has very naturally been supposed to uphold some kind of realistic views.[1] Tradition affirms that the question which gave rise to this sect had been discussed at the time of Buddha himself. If a division arises in a community with the result that some of its members are declared to be, or claim to be, realists, one would naturally be led to suppose that there were others who were non-realists, i.e. idealists of some kind. But, as a matter of fact, we do not meet with views definitely idealistic, i.e. with the denial of the existence of external objects, until a comparatively late date. Considering, on the other hand, that these would-be realists, like all Buddhists, denied the existence of a soul or a personality (*ātman*, *pudgala*), our uncertainty increases, and the suspicion arises that the battle between the Sarvāstivādins and their opponents was fought on an altogether different plane, about a question which had little to do with our conceptions of realism and idealism.[2]

[1] So Takakusu s.v. in *Hastings' Encyclopædia*. Mr. S. Z. Aung and Mrs. C. Rhys Davids, *Points of Controversy*, pp. 275–6, rightly observe that the question bears upon the existence of future and past *dharmas*, but this does not mean that "they believed in continued or immutable existence of everything". This would be drifting into Sānkhya doctrine, against which Buddhist philosophers were always uttering warnings; cf. Appendix I.

[2] The Buddhists themselves ascribe the origin of their idealistic philosophy to Vasubandhu; cf. my article in the Muséon, 1905, ii. But this was evidently only a revival of a tendency which, in a different form, was already revealed

The occasion upon which Buddha himself is supposed to have put forward the watchword "everything exists" was a discussion with the Ājīvikas, who flatly denied the influence of past deeds upon our destinies, since they were past and non-existent.[1] This sect upheld a kind of extreme determinism which served as excuse for moral incontinence; it maintained that "all things are inalterably fixed. There is no cause, either proximate or remote, for the depravity of being, or . . . for its purity . . . There is no such thing as power or energy or human exertion. Everything that thinks, has senses, is procreated, and lives, is destitute of force, power or energy. Their varying conditions, at any time, are due to fate, to their environment and their own nature".[2] Buddha's teaching, both in the moral domain and in ontology, was the reverse of this; it maintained moral responsibility and at the same time transformed all existing things into a congeries of subtle energies (*saṃskāra-samūha*). When pressed to say what was meant by the words "everything exists", he answered "everything exists means that the twelve *āyatanas* exist".[3] Now the twelve *āyatanas* are merely one of the many classifications of the elements of existence of matter and mind. The Sarvāstivādin school admitted seventy-five such elements. These elements were called *dharmas*. The full meaning of the term will emerge at the end of this article;

in the works of Açvaghoṣa and Nāgārjuna. *Ab. K.* bears witness that idealistic views were already discussed in the *Vibhāsā-çāstra*; cf. i, 42, Tibetan text, p. 77, 10, and Yaçomitra's comment.

[1] *Ab. K.* ad v, 24; cf. Appendix I.

[2] Cf. R. Hoernle's article in *Hastings' Encyclopædia*.

[3] This passage (*Saṃyuktāgama*, xiii, p. 16 (McGovern)) cannot be traced in the Pali Canon. Evidently the Theravādins suppressed it because it did not agree with their particular tenets. They accused the Vātsīputriyas of having suppressed the passages which ran against their views (*Soul Theory*, p. 840), and evidently did themselves the same. But even in their school the word *sabba* seems to have been used rather like a technical term. It did not mean "everything", but every item of the Buddhist table of elements. This table was supposed to be an "exhaustive division": cf. Mrs. Rhys Davids, *Buddhist Psychology*, p. 41; *Saṃyutta*, iv, 15–27; *Visuddhi-Magga*, ch. xiv; Warren, *Buddhism in translation*, p. 158; G. Grimm, *Buddhismus, passim.*

at present we take it to mean an ultimate entity, the conception of which, in the domain of matter, excludes the reality of everything except sense-data, and in the field of mind, of everything except separate mental phenomena. We will begin by reviewing the different kinds of elements and their various classifications, and then proceed to determine what was the Buddhist conception of an element of existence. This will lead us to ascertain more precisely in what sense the older Buddhist doctrine may have a claim to be called a realistic system.

II. Skandhas

The simplest classification of all elements of existence is represented by a division into five groups of elements: (1) matter, (2) feelings, (3) ideas, (4) volitions and other faculties, and (5) pure sensation or general consciousness.[1] If we realize that the group of matter represents no other matter than sense-data, that a soul is excluded and replaced by feelings, ideas, volitions, and pure sensation, we cannot but be surprised that from under a cover of Oriental terminology an epitome of matter and mind emerges which very nearly approaches the standpoint of modern European science.

Three of these groups, namely, feelings, ideas, and pure sensation, contain one element (*dharma*) each. They are, nevertheless, called groups because they include feelings, etc., as past, present, and future, proximate and remote, external and internal, morally pure or impure, etc.[2] The group of matter includes ten elements, ten different varieties of sense-data.[3] The group of volitions, etc., includes fifty-eight elements, various mental faculties and general forces.[4]

[1] The reasons for these renderings of the terms *rūpa*, *vedanā*, *saṃjñā*, *saṃskāra*, and *vijñāna* will be given later on.

[2] *Ab. K.*, i, 20.

[3] Ibid., i, 14.

[4] All the *saṃskāras* except *vedanā* and *saṃjñā*, ibid., i, 15. The three eternal elements—*asaṃskṛta*—are not included in the *skandhas*, ibid., i, 22. Together with *avijñapti-rūpa* this will make seventy-five elements in all.

The physical elements of a personality, including its outer world—the external objects—are represented in this classification by one item—matter;[1] the mental ones are distributed among the four others.

For "Matter and Mind" the old, pre-Buddhistic term *nāma-rūpa* is used, where *rūpa* represents the elements of matter and *nāma* includes the four mental classes.

But the most general division of all elements is into matter (*rūpa*), mind (*citta-caitta*), and forces (*saṃskāra*). The fourth group (*saṃskāra-skandha*), which includes mental faculties and general forces, is here split into two parts; the mental faculties are then united to all other mental groups, and are brought under the head of mind; the general forces or energies receive a separate place (*citta-viprayukta-saṃskāra*).[2] This threefold division is very popular and known in Mongolia and Tibet to every schoolboy.[3]

III. Āyatanas

A second, more detailed, classification of the elements is made with a view to a division into cognitive faculties and their objects. There are six cognitive faculties and six categories of corresponding objects. They make the twelve *āyatanas* or "bases" of cognition, viz. :—

I. Six internal bases (*adhyātma-āyatana*) or receptive faculties (*indriya*).	II. Six external bases (*bāhya-āyatana*) or objects (*viṣaya*).
1. Sense of vision (*cakṣur-indriya-āyatana*).	7. Colour and shape (*rūpa-āyatana*).
2. Sense of audition (*çrotr-endriya-āyatana*).	8. Sound (*çabda-āyatana*).

[1] Among the physical elements there is one called *avijñapti* which broadly corresponds to what we might call the moral character of a person: for some special reasons it is entered by the Sarvāstivādins in their physical class (*rūpa*), but other schools include it in mind (*Ab. K.*, i, 11). In the *āyatana* and *dhātu* classifications it is included not in the physical items, but in the general class *dharmāḥ*, i.e. *āyatana* or *dhātu* No. 12. In the following account we leave this special element unnoticed, cf. Appendix II, under *Matter*.

[2] Or a slightly differing fivefold division: *rūpa*, *citta*, *caitta*, *viprayukta-saṃskāra*, and *nirvāṇa*; cf. *Ab. K.*, ii, 22, and Appendix II.

[3] *Zugs-çes-ldan-min-hdu-byed.*

3. Sense of smelling (*ghrāṇ-endriya-āyatana*).
4. Sense of taste (*jihv-endriya-āyatana*).
5. Sense of touch (*kāy-endriya-āyatana*).
6. Faculty of the intellect or consciousness (*mana-indriya-āyatana*).
9. Odour (*gandha-āyatana*).
10. Taste (*rasa-āyatana*).
11. Tangibles (*spraṣṭavya-āyatana*).
12. Non-sensuous objects (*dharma-āyatana* or *dharmāḥ*).

In this classification the eleven first items correspond to eleven elements (*dharma*), each including one. The twelfth item contains all the remaining sixty-four elements, and it is therefore called *dharma-āyatana* or simply *dharmāḥ*, i.e. the *remaining* elements.

The term *āyatana* means "entrance" (*āyaṃ tanoti*). It is an "entrance" for consciousness and mental phenomena (*citta-caittānām*). Consciousness, it is stated, never arises alone, since it is pure sensation, without any content. It is always supported or "introduced" by two elements: a cognitive faculty and a corresponding objective element. These are the supporters or the "doors" (*dvāra*) for consciousness to appear. Visual consciousness (*cakṣur-vijñāna*) arises in correlation (*pratītya*) with the sense of vision (*cakṣur-indriya*) and some colour (*rupaṃ ca*). In the case of the sixth cognitive faculty (*manas*), consciousness itself, i.e. its preceding moment, acts as a faculty for apprehending non-sensuous objects.

The trend of this classification, which is a characteristic feature of Buddhism from its very beginnings, is unmistakable. It intends to give a division of all objects of cognition into sense-objects and non-sensuous ones. The first are then divided into ten groups according to the five senses and their five objects, and the second (*dharma-āyatana*, or simply *dharmāḥ*), including every non-sensuous object, is left undivided. There are six items corresponding to six cognitive faculties. Thus the twelve *āyatanas*, or "bases of cognition", represent all elements of existence distributed within six subjective and six corresponding objective items. Their synonym is "everything" (*sarvam*). When the principle "everything exists" is set forth it has the meaning that nothing but the twelve bases of cognition are existent. An object which cannot be viewed as a *separate* object of cognition or a *separate* faculty of cognition is unreal, as e.g. the soul, or the personality. Being a congeries of separate elements it is declared to be a name, and not a reality, not a *dharma*.[1]

IV. Dhātus

The division of the elements of existence into eighteen *dhātus*, although very similar—it represents, indeed, in its first twelve items a repetition of the former one—is taken from a quite different view-point. Buddhist philosophy is an analysis of separate elements, or forces, which unite in the production of one stream (*saṃtāna*) of events. The unphilosophic mind of common people supposes this stream to represent a personality or an individual (*pudgala*). Viewed as components of such a stream, the elements are called *dhātus*. Just as different metals (*dhātus*) might be extracted out of a mine, just so does the stream of an individual life reveal elements of eighteen different kinds (*dhātu* = *gotra*).[2] It always includes six faculties (from *cakṣur-dhātu* up to *mano-dhātu*), six kinds of objective elements (from *rūpa-dhātu* up to *dharma-dhātu*), and six kinds of consciousness, beginning with visual consciousness, or visual sensation (*cakṣur-vijñāna-dhātu*), and ending with consciousness purely mental, i.e. non-sensuous (*mano-vijñāna-dhātu*). Thus, in addition to the twelve components corresponding to the twelve bases of cognition, we have :—

[1] The right explanation of the term *āyatana* is given in O. Rosenberg's *Problems*, p. 138 ff. The usual translation "sphere" ignores the *fundamentum divisionis*. S. Z. Aung, *Compendium*, p. 256, although containing the right suggestion, thinks it "might well be left untranslated".

[2] *Ab. K.*, i, 20. It may be noted that the number of component elements (*tattvas*) of the rudimentary body in Sānkhya is likewise eighteen. That the term *dhātu* has been borrowed from medical science, where it means element of the body, can hardly be doubted.

13. Visual consciousness (*cakṣur-vijñāna-dhātu*).
14. Auditory „ (*çrotra-vijñāna-dhātu*).
15. Olfactory „ (*ghrāṇa-vijñāna-dhātu*).
16. Gustatory „ (*jihvā-vijñāna-dhātu*).
17. Tactile „ (*kāya-vijñāna-dhātu*)
18. Non-sensuous „ (*mano-vijñāna-dhātu*).

Consciousness, which is but one element (*dharma*), is split in this classification into seven items, since it enters into the composition of an individual life as a faculty (*mano-dhātu*) and as six different kinds of sensations, differentiated by their origin, as from one of the senses, or from a purely mental non-sensuous source.[1]

All these varieties of consciousness exist only in the ordinary plane of existence (*kāma-Dhātu*). In higher worlds (*rūpa-Dhātu*) sense-consciousness gradually disappears, in the immaterial worlds (*arūpa-Dhātu*) only non-sensuous consciousness is left. A division of consciousness into various kinds (*dhātu* 13–18) is thus made necessary for the composition of formulas of elements corresponding to the denizens of various worlds.[2]

We will now proceed to consider the separate elements in the order of their most general classification into Matter, Mind, and Forces.

[1] *Dhātu* is often defined just as *dharma*: *sva-svabhāva-dhāraṇāt*, or *sva-lakṣaṇa-dhāraṇāt* (cf. S. Z. Aung, *Compendium*, p. 255 ff.), but this is only partly correct, since the *dhātu* No. 12 includes sixty-four *dharmas*, and the seven *dhātus*, No. 6 and Nos. 13–18, correspond to one single *dharma*—the *vijñāna* (=*manas*=*cittam*). The definition in *Ab. K.*, i, 20, is *dhātu*=*gotra*. We can, accordingly, translate *dhātu* by "component", "element", or "class of elements", just as the case may require.

[2] When the three *Dhātus* are mentioned the term *Dhātu* means world (*loka*) or plane of existence (*avacara*). It has nothing to do with the eighteen *dhātus*. The worlds are divided into material (*rūpa-*) and immaterial (*arūpa-*) worlds, the former again into worlds of carnal desire or defiled matter—*kāma-*(*rūpa*)*-Dhātu*, and those of pure, or reduced, matter—(*niṣkāma-*) *rūpa-Dhātu*. In the *kāma-Dhātu* life consists of eighteen components (*dhātus*), in the *rūpa-Dhātu* of fourteen (excepted are Nos. 9–10 and 15–16), in the *arūpa-Dhātu* of three (Nos. 6, 12, and 18). In *rūpa-* and *arūpa-Dhātus* life is characterized by different degrees of perpetual trance (*dhyāna*). Ordinary people can be transferred into these higher regions of trance either through being reborn in them (*utpatti*) or through an effort of transic meditation (*samāpatti*).

V. Elements of Matter

Matter (*rūpa*) or the physical elements (*rūpiṇo dharmāḥ*), which in the first classification occupied one item (*rūpa-skandha*), is otherwise distributed into ten items (Nos. 1–5 and 7–11). The term *rūpa-āyatana* is reserved for visible matter or, more precisely, the phenomenon of visibility alone, this being matter *par excellence*.[1] The general characteristic of matter, or material elements, is impenetrability (*sa-pratighatva*), which is defined as the fact that space occupied by one of them cannot, at the same time, be occupied by another.[2]

The elements of visibility are divided into two main groups, colours and shapes. There are eight colours and twelve different shapes. Another theory reduces all colours to two, light and darkness. All other varieties of visibility are represented as differences of lines. The opposite view, namely, that colours alone are realities and shapes (*saṃsthāna*) represent constructions of the mind (*mānasam, parikalpitam*) (superimposed upon the difference of coloration as an interpretation of it), was favoured by the Sautrāntikas.[3] A line, say a line drawn by the motion of the hand, being an

[1] *Ab. K.*, i, 24.

[2] The etymological explanation is: *rūpyata iti rūpam*, i.e. matter is what materializes. Different meanings are then given of this materializing: pressure, pain, disappearance, or change. Thus matter is something that disappears. The real meaning is impenetrability (*sa-pratighatva*), which is further variously explained. Kumāralābha gives to the phenomenon of impenetrability an idealistic interpretation: "the impossibility for the intellect to imagine the presence of two such objects occupying the same space" (ibid., Tibetan text, p. 50, 17 ff.). Professor O. Rosenberg strongly objects to the interpretation of *rūpa* as matter. He maintains that Buddhism from its very outset viewed the phenomenal world as an illusion and relegated every reality to some transcendental world (cf. *Problems*, chap. x). He suggests "sense-elements" for *rūpa*. This would find a place in an idealistic system and would be supported by the above interpretation of Kumāralābha. But it is, evidently, not the view adopted by the school of the Sarvāstivādins. It is true that there is no other matter than sense-data. This should not prevent us, just as it does not prevent modern philosophers who favour the same view, from using the term "matter" for facts characterized by impenetrability.

[3] *Ab. K.*, i, 10, and Yaç. comment.

intimation of something (*vijñapti*), is an element (*rūpa-dharma*) of length [1]; the line of the flight of a bird in the air is the same. They are interpreted as the apparitions of the element of length or of some colour, and all Buddhist matter must be conceived according to this pattern. They are material elements without any matter in them.

A glance at the ten items corresponding to matter in the *āyatana*-division will convince us that no other matter except sense-data is recognized. It is broadly divided into two categories, objective sense-data (*viṣaya*) constituting external objects, and sense-organs (*indriya*) conceived as a kind of translucent subtle *matter* which covers the body when it is living. This division reminds us of the Sānkhya view that matter developed along two different lines, the one with predominance of the translucent intelligence-stuff (*sattva*) resulting in sense-organs, the other, with predominance of dead matter (*tamas*), resulting in sense-objects in their subtle (*tan-mātra*) and gross (*mahābhūta*) forms. In fact the concept of *tan-mātra* comes very near to the Buddhist conception of an element of matter (*rūpa-dharma*). The fundamental difference between the two conceptions is that in the Sānkhya system these elements are modifications or appurtenances of an eternal substance. In Buddhism they are mere sense-data without any substance.

The translucent matter of the sense-organs (*rūpa-prasāda*) is very subtle; it is like the shining of a jewel, it cannot be cut in two,[2] it cannot be burnt,[3] it has no weight,[4] and it disappears without a residue at death.[5] It is, nevertheless,

[1] *Ab. K.*, i, 10, Tib. text, p. 17.

[2] If a member, or all members, are chopped off the body, the sense-organ-matter is not cut even in two parts, i.e. the parts that are cut off are senseless. The movements of a lizard's tail after it is knocked off the main body are explained not by the presence of this life-matter (*indriya*), but by the intensification of the *vāyu* element, i.e. it is a lifeless process (*Ab. K.*, i, 36, Tibetan text, p. 63, and Yaç. comment).

[3] *Ab. K.*, i, 36, Tib. text, p. 63, 13. [4] Ibid.

[5] *Ab. K.*, i, 37, and Yaç. comment: *mṛtasya ananuvṛtteḥ*. This is a point of analogy with the *linga-çarīra* of the Sānkhyas.

atomic, and is represented by five different kinds of atoms. The atoms of the organ of sight (*cakṣur-indriya*) cover in concentric circles the eye-ball. The atoms of the organ of taste, or, more precisely, that matter which is supposed to convey the sensation of taste, covers in concentric semicircles the tongue. The atoms of the organ of touch (*kāy-endriya*) cover the whole body.[1] The idea that all these different kinds of special matter are, indeed, the same translucent subtle stuff covering the whole living body and disappearing at death had also its advocates, who consequently reduced all senses to one, the sense of touch, but this did not find general acceptance. Being as subtle as the shining of a jewel, this matter cannot appear alone; it is supported by gross matter (*mahābhūta*), of which the eye-ball and flesh in general consist.

The atoms of external matter are likewise divided into atoms of general, universal, or fundamental matter, and special atoms of colour-, sound-, tangibility-matter, etc. The fundamental elements are four in number; they are manifested by the facts of hardness or repulsion, cohesion or attraction, heat and motion.[2] Conventionally they are called earth, water, fire, and air; but it is specified that these are only conventional appellations, and that in the name of the fourth general element (*īraṇa*) alone both the technical and the usual meanings coalesce, because the word *īraṇa* has both the significations of motion and air as well.[3] The fact that the fourth element is motion is an indication of the trend of this division; the general elements of matter, like all Buddhist elements, are more forces than substances. These four elements appear always together, always in equal proportion. There is as much element of heat in a blazing flame as there is in wood or in water, and vice versa, the difference is only in their intensity.[4] The general elements of matter (*mahābhūta*)

[1] *Ab. K.*, i, 44, Tibetan text, p. 84, 15 ff.

[2] *Ab. K.*, i, 12. [3] *Ab. K.*, i, 13.

[4] e.g. the tactile sensation may have a different degree of intensity as the touch by a bunch of steel needles is more intensely felt than the touch of a painter's brush, although the quantity may be the same. The existence

are brought under the head of tangibles (*āyatana* No. 11). Since there is only a limited number of general manifestations of tangibility, therefore their number is four.[1] There is, apparently, a distinction between the elements in themselves and their manifestations, because the four facts of resistance, attraction, heat, and motion are clearly called manifestations (*lakṣaṇa*) of the elements (*dharma*), which, accordingly. must be something different, something mysterious or transcendental, similar in this respect to the *guṇas* of the Sāṅkhyas. The other five kinds of objective matter (*āyatanas* Nos. 7–11) were not general, but special, corresponding to each of the five senses; the tangibility-matter alone (*āyatana* No. 11 includes both the general (*mahābhūta*) and the special (*bhautika*) elements of matter.[2] They were also atomic, but could not appear independently without being combined with the fundamental ones, in the ratio of four atoms of primary matter to one of secondary. Thus the minimum number of atoms indispensable for their actual appearance in life was eight: four atoms of general materiality combined with each atom of colour, odour, taste, and secondary tangibility-matter (such as smoothness, coarseness, etc.). If the particular piece of matter resounded, atoms of sound were added and the combination consisted then of nine different atoms.[3] The combined atoms (*saṅghāta-paramāṇu*) alone appear in phenomenal reality, the simple ones, or infra-atomic elements, presumably, were relegated to transcendental reality, in accordance with the general character

of cohesiveness, i.e. of the element "water" in a flame, is proved by its keeping a shape; the presence of repulsion, i.e. of the element "earth". in water, is proved by the fact of its supporting a ship, etc. (cf. *Ab. K.*, ii, 22, and Yaçom.).

[1] *Ab. K.*, i, 35, Tibetan text, p. 61, 5 ff.

[2] Ibid.

[3] The actual number of atoms in a *saṅghāta-paramāṇu* will be much greater, since each atom of secondary (*bhautika*) matter needs a set of four primary atoms of its own, but if *dhātus* alone are reckoned the number will express the classes (*dhātu*) of elements (*dharma*) represented (cf. *Ab. K.*, ii, 22).

of a Buddhist element. This device made it an easy task for Buddhists to oppose the indivisibility of atoms.[1]

VI. Elements of Mind

In the *āyatana* classification two items (Nos. 6 and 12) are devoted to the elements of mind (*citta-caitta-dharmāḥ*, *arūpiṇo dharmāḥ*) and, according to the principle of this classification, they represent two correlative groups: a subjective one (*indriya*) and an objective one (*viṣaya*). The principle of externality of one element in regard to another, i.e. the idea of separate elements (*pṛthag-dharma*), is maintained in the field of mind just as in the field of matter. Mind is split into two chief parts. The subjective part, or mind viewed as a receptive faculty, is represented by one element called, indiscriminately, *citta*, *vijñāna*, or *manas*.[2] It represents pure consciousness, or pure sensation, without any content. Its content is placed in the objective part which contains the definite sensation (*sparça*), feelings (*vedanā*), ideas (*sanjñā*), volitions (*cetanā*), and various other mental phenomena up to the number of forty-six separate elements.[3] So it is that feelings come to be viewed as objects of the mind, a position which, for other reasons, they likewise possess in the Sānkhya system. The category in which they are entered is called the (general) group of elements (*dharma-āyatana*) or simply "the elements" (*dharmāḥ*). As stated above, the first eleven "bases" contain one element (*dharma*) each, but this last one contains the remaining sixty-four elements of the list. Beside the forty-six mental phenomena it contains the fourteen elementary forces (*viprayukta-saṃskāra*), the element of character (*avijñapti*) and the three eternal elements (*asaṃskṛta*): among the latter is Nirvāṇa, the chief *dharma*.

[1] *Ab. K.*, i, 43, Tibetan text, p. 83.

[2] *Ab. K.*, ii, 34. The same terms in the Pali Canon, *Saṃyutta*, ii, 94.

[3] The Theravāda reckoned fifty-one. Cf. the fifty *bhāvas* of the Sānkhyas, some of them exhibiting an analogy with corresponding Buddhist *caitta-dharmas*. A full list of the forty-six *caitta-dharmas* is given below, App. II.

For this reason the term " elements " (*dharmāḥ*) is a sufficient indication of this group, because the other categories, although also containing elements (*dharmāḥ*), have a special name each.[1] The common feature of all these elements is that they are apprehended by the intellect directly without any intermediate agency of the senses. In the apprehension of sense-objects there is likewise participation by the intellect; but these *dharmāḥ* are non-sensuous objects, they are the exclusive domain of the receptive intellect, just as colour is the exclusive domain of the sense of vision.[2] The definition of receptive consciousness is pregnant: *vijñānam prativijñaptiḥ*, i.e. " consciousness is an intimation, or awareness, in every single case " (of what is now present to the senses, or to the mind directly).[3] If an apprehension contains some, albeit quite indefinite, content, say some indefinite visual sensation, it will then

[1] Every *āyatana* is thus a *dharmāyatana*, but No. 12 is *dharmāyatana* par excellence. Just so is it that the ten material *āyatanas* all include matter. They are, consequently, all of them, *rūpāyatanas*. But only one of them—the visible element, *āyatana* No. 7—retains the name of *rūpāyatana* as its special designation, because it represents the most characteristic and important among the elements of matter. Cf. *Ab. K.*, i, 24, Tibetan text, p. 42, 17 ff.

[2] Prof. and Mrs. Geiger, op. cit., p. 80, have established for the *dharmāḥ* in the technical sense the signification " the empirical things ". This is an example of the impotence of the "philological method" ! It has not escaped their attention that *dharmāḥ* is synonymous with *dharmāyatana* and *dharmadhātu*, in which Nirvāṇa is included (p. 83), which is anything but empirical. The *dharmāḥ* are apprehended by *manaḥ* (p. 81), but the emphasis is put on the fact that they are apprehended *without the co-operation of the senses.* Everything is apprehended by *manaḥ*, but the *dharmāḥ* are external with regard to *manaḥ*; their place in the system is among the six *viṣaya*, as opposed to the six *indriya*, one of which, the sixth, is *manaḥ*. Concerning the meaning of the terms " external " and " internal " some remarks will be made later on, pp. 58–9, when discussing the theory of cognition.

[3] *Ab. K.*, i, 16. *Cittaṃ vijānāti*, Asl., p. 42 = " is aware *variously* " (M. Ting), must have the same import, if any. Cf. the Sānkhya definition of *pratyakṣa* in *Sānkhya-kārikā*, 5: *prativiṣay-ādhyavasāyo dṛṣṭam*, where we have likewise the distributive *prati-*, but *vijñāna* = *vijñaptiḥ*, since it is in the Sānkhya system represented by *puruṣa* (cf. below, Theory of Cognition, p. 63), is replaced by *adhyavasāya*—the function of the internal organ (synthesis).

represent the next degree, a real sensation (*sparça*).[1] The definite perception (*parichitti*) of a colour will be an "idea" (*sanjñā*), but consciousness as the perceptive faculty is pure sensation. Although quite undifferentiated in itself, this pure sensation is, nevertheless, distinguished from the standpoint of its origin or, more precisely, its environment, i.e. the elements by which its appearance is accompanied. From this point of view, as stated above, there is a set of six different kinds (*dhātu*) of consciousness, corresponding to a set of six receptive faculties and a set of six kinds of objects. We thus have six categories of consciousness (*ṣaḍ-vijñāna-kāyāḥ*), beginning with visual sensation or, more precisely, pure sensation arising in connexion with some colour (*cakṣur-vijñāna-dhātu*) and ending with consciousness accompanying a non-sensuous object (*mano-vijñāna-dhātu*). We have besides the same consciousness as a receptive faculty (*dhātu* No. 6). As a receptive faculty *mano-dhātu* is not different from consciousness arising in connexion with abstract objects (*mano-vijñāna-dhātu*); it is the same reality, the same *dharma*. But for symmetrical arrangement it has been found necessary to have a set of three items for the purely mental elements, just as there is a threefold set of faculty, object, and sensation corresponding to each of the senses.[2] The difference between consciousness as a receptive faculty and the same consciousness accompanying an abstract object is then said to be a difference of time. Consciousness in the role corresponding to the place occupied in the system by the senses is the consciousness of the preceding moment.[3] The Theravādins, evidently for the same purpose of symmetrical arrangement, introduced into

[1] Three *dharmas* are engaged when this kind of sensation, sometimes translated as "contact", is produced: *trayāṇāṃ sannipātaḥ sparçaḥ* (*tiṇṇaṃ saṃgati phasso*): the consciousness (*citta*), the sense-organ, and the sense-object. Cf. below under theory of cognition.

[2] *Ab. K.*, i, 16, Tibetan text, p. 29, l. 17.

[3] The mental phenomena (*caitta-dharma*) also have their objects; they are according to the current terminology *sālambana*, but they are themselves *viṣaya* and not *indriya* (*Ab. K.*, i, 34, cf. Tibetan text, p. 49, l. 19).

the system a "heart-stuff" (*hadaya-vatthu*) which supports the non-sensuous cognitions, just as the other sense-stuffs "support" sense-cognitions. It occupies in the system the place of the sixth organ (*āyatana* or *dhātu* No. 6).[1]

Although external in regard to one another, consciousness and mental phenomena (*citta-caitta*) were conceived as being in a closer, more intimate, connexion than other combining elements. Pure sensation (*citta*) could never appear in life in its true separate condition; it was always accompanied by some secondary mental phenomena (*caitta*).[2] Among these mental phenomena (*caitta-dharma*) or faculties (*saṃskāra*) three are especially conspicuous, namely, feelings (*vedanā*), ideas (*sanjñā*), and volitions (*cetanā*). In the classification into groups (*skandha*) they occupy three separate items, all the remaining ones being included together with the volitions in the *saṃskāra-skandha*. Feelings (*vedanā*) are defined as emotions pleasant, unpleasant, or neutral.[3] Ideas (*sanjña*) are defined as operations of abstract thought, as that which "abstracts" (*udgrahaṇa*) a common characteristic sign (*nimitta*) from the individual objects.[4] Even the definite representation (*parichitti*) of a colour is brought under this head.[4] It is exactly what in later Indian philosophy, Buddhist as well as Brahmanical, was understood by "definite" (*sa-vikalpaka*) cognition. Dignāga and Dharmakīrti introduced into Indian logic the distinction between pure sense knowledge, free from any operation of abstract thought (*kalpanāpoḍha*), and definite cognition (*sa-vikalpaka*).[5] It was then adopted by Uddyotakara and

[1] Cf. Mrs. C. Rhys Davids, *B. Psych.*, pp. 32, 70. This heart-stuff had, presumably, as little to do with the actual heart as the *cakṣur-indriya*-stuff with the actual eye. Indian medical science assumed the existence of a subtle *ākāça*-food-stuff as a vehicle of mental processes. It is here called heart-stuff.

[2] *Ab. K.*, ii, 23.

[3] *Ab. K.*, i, 14.

[4] Ibid.

[5] Cf. the definition of *pratyakṣa* in *Nyāyā-bindu* 1.

the whole of the Nyāya-Vaiçeṣika school.[1] It now appears that Dignāga was not the originator of this doctrine, he only adapted it to his system. From the very beginning Buddhism had established this difference: *vijñāna* and its synonyms *citta, manaḥ* represent pure sensation, the same as the *kalpanāpoḍha pratyakṣa* of Dignāga, and *sanjñā* corresponds to definite ideas. Every construction (*kalpanā*), every abstraction (*udgrahaṇa*),[2] every definite (*parichinna*) representation, such as blue and yellow, long and short, male and female, friend and enemy, happy and miserable—this is all brought under the head of ideas (*sanjñā*) as distinguished from *vijñāna* = pure sensation.

Volition (*cetanā*) is defined as the mental effort that precedes action. It is an element or a force which enters in the composition of a personal life (*santāna*). It must not be forgotten that, since there is no personality in the Buddhist outlook of the universe, there certainly is no will in our sense, i.e. no personal will. There is a certain arrangement of elements, there is an element, or a force, or, still more precisely, the simple fact (*dharma*) that the elements are arranged in a certain way, according to certain laws. This fact is pointed to by the term *cetanā*. It " arranges " (*sancetayati*) [3] the elements in " streams ", which simple folk deem to be personalities. It is synonymous with the law of moral causation (*karma*) [4] and likewise with the force of vitality, the " élan vital " (*bhāvanā, vāsanā*), which in the Buddhist system replaces any conscious agent, whether soul or God or even a conscious

[1] Cf. *Nyāyā-vārttika, pratyakṣa-sūtra.*

[2] *Udgrahaṇa* is literally " abstraction ", *kalpanā* " imagination ", " construction ". It corresponds to the part taken in Kant's system by " productive imagination ", whereas *vijñāna*, or the *pratyakṣa* of Dignāga, corresponds to " reine Sinnlichkeit ". Cf. my *Logic of later Buddhists* (chapter on *kalpanā*).

[3] To be derived from the root *ci* from which the Buddhists derive *citta* as well (Asb., p. 63); *sancetayati* is exactly, in form and meaning, the Russian *sochetayeti*; the Pāli *abhisandahati* has the same import, cf. S. Z. Aung, *Compendium*, p. 235.

[4] The definition of *karma* is *cetanā cetayitvā ca karaṇam*, *Ab. K.*, iv, 1 ff., the same as in *Anguttara*, iii, 415; cf. Mrs. C. Rhys Davids, *B. Psych.*, p. 93.

human being.[1] A moment of this kind of will accompanies every conscious moment (*citta*).

There are, on the whole, ten mental elements which accompany every conscious moment; they are called the "general" mental elements.[2] There are ten others which are particularly "favourable" for progress towards the final appeasement of life; they are faith, courage, equanimity, etc. Ten others have the contrary unfavourable or oppressive (*kliṣṭa*) character. There are some others which have no definite moral character. All these mental elements are not general; they accompany only some of the moments of consciousness, not all of them.[3]

VII. Forces

The definitions of the will (*cetanā*) and of the force (*saṃskāra*) are indeed the same, "what produces the manifestations (*abhi-saṃskaroti*) of combining elements (*saṃskṛtam*)"[4]: it is a "concerted agency".[5] Since all forces are agencies acting in some combination with other elements, we may in rendering this conception, for the sake of expediency, safely drop the word "combining" and use "forces" alone.[6] There are some indications that originally there was only one *saṃskāra* in the Buddhist system, the will, and that gradually a whole catalogue of them was developed, some of the elements being entered into this group rather forcibly, with excuses.[7] The

[1] *Ab. K.*, ix, *Soul Theory*, p. 942.

[2] *Citta-mahābhūmika.*

[3] A full list of them will be found in O. Rosenberg's *Problems*, p. 374, and at the end of this book.

[4] This definition we find already in the oldest sources, e.g. *Saṃyutta*, iii, 87, and it is repeated in numberless passages of the *Ab. K.*; cf. S. Z. Aung, *Compendium*, p. 236.

[5] *Sambhūya-kāritvam, Ab. K.*, i, 7.

[6] This the Buddhists themselves have also done in replacing *saṃskṛta* by *kṛtaka*, cf. *Nyāyab. ṭīkā*, pp. 47, 50, etc. A unity, without combining, can produce nothing: *na kiṃcid ekam ekasmāt* (Dignāga).

[7] In the *Ab. K.*, i, 15, there is an interesting effort to prove that all *saṃskāras* (sixty) are included in the *saṃskāra-skandha* and not *cetanā* alone, as it would be possible to conclude from scriptural passages. As the second member of the chain of causation, *saṃskāra* is equivalent to *karma*.

most typical forces are the four forces of origination and decay, etc., which accompany every other element in life. Some details concerning them will be given in the sequel. In general, all elements may be divided into substances and forces (*dravya* and *saṃskāra*). The forces are then divided into mental faculties, with the will as chief among them, and non-mental (*citta-viprayukta*) forces, among which the origination and decay forces are the most typical. But even these latter forces are sometimes given a certain amount of substantiality (*dravyatopi santi*).[1] The word and conception *saṃskāra* performs a conspicuous part in all Indian philosophical systems. It usually means some latent mysterious power, which later on reveals itself in some patent fact. It sometimes is identified with the "unknown" (*adṛṣṭa*) conceived as a force *sui generis*. Since every philosophy is but a search for the hidden reality as opposed to the patent surface of life, the importance of the conception of a *saṃskāra* is quite natural. Every system had its own definition and scope attributed to the connotation of this term. The Ājīvika sect, as we have seen, was known by its denial of the existence of such forces. The Buddhists, on the contrary, converted all their elements into subtle forces of some degree. The subtler the element the more was it given the character of a force; but even the coarsest elements, the *mahābhūtas*, look more like forces than substances. There is a constant fluctuation in Buddhist terminology between a force (*saṃskāra*) and a substance influenced by these forces (*saṃskṛta*). A force, it must be recalled, should not be regarded as a real influence of something extending beyond its own existence in order to penetrate into another—this would be

Mrs. C. Rhys Davids calls my attention to the following very illuminating words in *Saṃyutta*, iii, 60: *Katamā ca bhikkhave saṅkhārā? Cha-y-ime cetanākāyā rūpa-sadda-gandha-rasa-phaṭṭhabba-sañcetanā dhammasañcetanā ime vuccanti saṅkhārā.* According to Yaçomitra, l.c., the mental faculties are included in the *saṃskāra-skandha* because they obey the will, the other forces because they are similar to the will (*cetanā*).

[1] *Ab. K.*, ii, 2, 24.

upakāra—but simply as a condition, a fact, upon which another fact arises or becomes prominent (*utkarṣa*) by itself —this is *saṃskāra* in the Buddhist system.[1]

The little we know of the history of Indian philosophy induces us to look to the Sānkhya system as the foundation of scientific thinking. In that school the fundamental ideas were formed which sometimes unconsciously affected all later constructions. What do we find there? Three fundamental principles, Matter, Mind-stuff, and Energy-stuff, as interdependent moments in every real and substantial existence. Even energy is substantial in this sense. The infinitesimals of energy, present everywhere, are semi-material; although different from the inertia of Matter, and the luminosity of Mind, they are separate and substantial.[2] The Buddhist elements as infinitesimal realities, divided into elements of Matter, Mind, and Forces, look like a reply to the Sānkhya constructions from an architect of greater skill: "you maintain the realities are *guṇas*, we say they are *dharmas*." The fundamental idea of infinitesimal realities may be recognized in the *dharmas*, the idea of forces everywhere present can be traced to its origin in the Sānkhya conception of *rajas*; there are forces which are different from matter and mind (*rūpa-citta-viprayukta*). A pluralistic view of the whole is added to make the originality of the new system, in contrast to the unitarian tendency of the old one. But, be the case as it may, every element of matter and mind may be called in Buddhism a *samskāra*, which, in this case, will stand for *saṃskṛta-dharma*.[3] The Buddhist idea of a force

[1] Cf. the *paribhāṣās* to *Pāṇini*, ii, 3, 53; vi, 1, 139; and iv, 2, 16; iv, 4, 3, in the *Kāçikā* (not occurring in the *M. bhāṣya*). Cf. below, p. 69.

[2] Cf. B. Seal, *The Positive Sciences of the Hindus*, and S. Dasgupta, *The Study of Patañjali*. The interpretation of the *guṇas* given there is entirely based on Vyasa who, as will be seen below, p. 46, was strongly influenced by *abhidharma*. Concerning their *mythological* origin cf. Senart, *J. As.* 1915, v. ii, pp. 151 ff.

[3] Yaçomitra (*Ab. K.*, i, 15) remarks that the name *saṃskṛta* is given in anticipation, since an element will become *saṃskṛta* only when the forces (*saṃskāra*) shall have exhibited their efficiency. In the popular formula *anityāḥ sarve saṃskārāḥ* the word *saṃskāra* stands for *saṃskṛta-dharma*.

seems to be that it is the subtle form of a substance, but even substance is here subtle enough. The order in which the elements appear in the first classification into groups is interpreted as a gradual progress from coarseness to subtlety; matter (*rūpa*) is coarser than feeling (*vedanā*), feeling more palpable than ideas (*sanjñā*), the remaining energies (*saṃskāra*) still more subtle.[1]

The pure forces (*viprayukta-saṃskāra*) are the most subtle among the elements. In the loftiest, highest worlds, where existence is entirely spiritualized, their agency continues; they are the last to be suppressed before final extinction is reached. The chief among them are the four forces of origination and destruction, etc., which are the very essence of every existence. Then there are two forces, *prāpti* and *aprāpti*, which are supposed to control the collection of elements composing a personal life or to prevent (*aprāpti*) the appearance in it of an element that is not in agreement with its general character. The Sautrāntikas and Vasubandhu deny the reality of these forces; for them they are mere names (*prajñapti*).[2] There are two forces supposed to be active in producing the highest degrees of trance—the unconscious trance (*asanjñi-samāpatti*) and the cessation (*nirodha-*) trance or catalepsy. They are also brought under the head of pure forces.[3] They evidently could not be brought under the head of mind, because consciousness at that time is supposed to be suppressed. Then there are three forces corresponding to the *sphoṭa* of other systems. All Indian systems contain speculations about the nature of sound, its physical as well as its significative aspect. The physical sound was in Buddhism considered, in agreement with the whole system, as a production, i.e. (flashing) of sound-atoms reposing on the atoms of fundamental matter. If

Saṃskāra etymologized as *karaṇa-sādhana* would mean force, and as *karma-sādhana* would be equal to *saṃskṛta-dharma*. The individual life, which consists of all these physical and mental elements and forces, is called *saṃskāra-samūhaḥ*, cf. Yaçom. (*Ab. K.*, ix). *sa cāpi Caitra-abhidhānaḥ saṃskāra-samūha-saṃtānaḥ*.

[1] *Ab. K.*, i, 22. [2] *Ab. K.*, ii, 37. [3] Ibid., ii, 46.

simultaneously some atoms of translucent sound matter (*çabda-rūpa-prasāda*) appeared in the ear, an auditory sensation (*çrotra-vijñāna*) was produced. But the significance of the sounds of speech was given by special forces. The Mīmāṃsaka school was known for its theory of transcendental, intelligible sounds which were eternal and ubiquitous, like Platonic ideas, and manifested themselves in the case of physical words being pronounced. Following their fundamental principle of analysing everything into minutest elements, the Buddhists imagined three separate forces which imparted to the sounds of speech their significativeness; the force of sound (*vyanjana*), which would seem to correspond to the modern idea of a "phonema", the force of words (*nāma*), and the force of sentences (*pada*).[1]

Generality, general ideas, are also conceived as a kind of force, and it is christened by the name of *nikāya-sabhāgatā*, a conception intended to replace by a "force" the substantial reality of the *sāmānya* of other systems.[2] In general this group of forces is a rather incongruous assemblage of elements which could not be placed elsewhere. As a separate group of elements it is absent in the Theravāda school. Some of its members seem to have found a place, for some reason, among the physical (*rūpa*) group of that school.[3]

VIII. Non-Substantiality of the Elements

After this succinct review of the elements of existence and their different classifications, we may consider the question as to what were they in their essence, what was the Buddhist

[1] *Ab. K.*, ii, 47 ff. *Vyanjana* here corresponds to *varṇa*, *nāma* to *sanjñā*, and *pada* to *vākya*, a case exhibiting clearly the desire to have a terminology of one's own, so common to Indian systems: "you maintain it in *sphoṭa*, we say it is *vyanjana-nāma-pada-saṃskāra*." The real existence of these forces is admitted by the Sarvāstivādin alone. For this reason they bring the Holy Scriptures under the head of *saṃskāra-skandha*, whereas the Sautrāntikas classify it under *rūpa*, as *çabda*, and the Vijñānavādins under *vijñāna-skandha*; cf. Vinītadeva's introduction to the *Santānāntara-siddhi*, edited by me in the *Bibl. Buddhica.*

[2] *Ab. K.*, ii, 41.

[3] Cf. S. Z. Aung, *Compendium*, p. 157.

conception of an element. The elements had four salient features: (1) they were not-substance—this refers to all the seventy-five elements, whether eternal or impermanent; (2) they had no duration—this refers only to the seventy-two impermanent elements of phenomenal existence; (3) they were unrest—this refers only to one part of the latter class, that which roughly corresponds to the ordinary man as opposed to the purified condition of the elements of a saint (*ārya*); and (4) their unrest had its end in final deliverance. Speaking technically: (1) all *dharmas* are *anātman*, (2) all *saṃskṛta-dharmas* are *anitya*, (3) all *sāsrava-dharmas* are *duḥkha*, and (4) their *nirvāṇa* alone is *çānta*. An element is non-substantial, it is evanescent, it is in a beginningless state of commotion, and its final suppression is the only Calm. These are what the Tibetans call the four "seals" of Buddha.[1] We now proceed to examine them separately.

Anātma

The term *anātman* is usually translated as "non-soul", but in reality *ātman* is here synonymous with a personality, an ego, a self, an individual, a living being, a conscious agent, etc.[2] The underlying idea is that, whatsoever be designated by all these names, it is not a real and ultimate fact, it is a mere name for a multitude of interconnected facts, which Buddhist philosophy is attempting to analyse by reducing them to real elements (*dharma*). Thus "soullessness" (*nairātmya*) is but the negative expression, indeed a synonym, for the existence of ultimate realities (*dharmatā*).[3] Buddhism

[1] The Southerns reckoned three "marks", evidently including the fourth in *duḥkha*, as its cessation; cf. S. Z. Aung, *Compendium*, p. 210.

[2] The whole issue with every detail is admirably expounded by Vasubandhu in a concluding, ninth, chapter of *Ab. K.*, translated in my *Soul Theory of the Bouddhists*. The terms *ātma*, *jīvan*, *sattva*, *pudgala* are here used as synonyms; cf. *Soul Theory*, p. 838, and *Kathāvatthu-atthakathā*, p. 8. The Vātsīputrīyas made some difference between *pudgala* and *ātman*; they were *pudgalavādins*, but not *ātmavādins*. Although admitting a limited, very shady, reality of *pudgala*, they denied it the ultimate reality of a *dharma*; cf. *Soul Theory* and below, p. 70 ff.

[3] *Pravacanadharmatā punar atra nairātmyam buddhānuçāsanī vā*, Yaçom. ad *Ab. K.*, ix, in fine.

never denied the existence of a personality, or a soul, in the empirical sense, it only maintained that it was no ultimate reality (not a *dharma*). The Buddhist term for an individual, a term which is intended to suggest the difference between the Buddhist view and other theories, is *santāna*, i.e. a "stream", viz. of interconnected facts. It includes the mental elements and the physical ones as well, the elements of one's own body and the external objects, as far as they constitute the experience of a given personality. The representatives of eighteen classes (*dhātu*) of elements combine together to produce this interconnected stream. There is a special force, called *prāpti,* which holds these elements combined. It operates only within the limits of a single stream and not beyond. This stream of elements kept together, and not limited to present life, but having its roots in past existences and its continuation in future ones—is the Buddhist counterpart of the Soul or the Self of other systems.

Consequent upon the denial of substance is the denial of every difference between the categories of substance and quality. There is no "inherence" of qualities in substance; in this respect all real elements are equally independent. As separate entities they then become substances *sui generis.* "Whatsoever exists is a substance," says Vasubandhu.[1] "An element is something having an essence of its own,"[2] is the current definition. To every unit of quality there is a corresponding subtle element (*dharma*) which either directly manifests itself or, according to the Sarvāstivādins, remaining for ever a transcendental reality, produces a reaction (*kāritva, lakṣaṇa*) which we wrongly interpret as being a quality. All sense-data (*rūpa*) are substances in that sense that there is no stuff they belong to. If we say "earth *has* odour, etc.", it is only an inadequate expression; we ought to say "earth *is* odour, etc.", since beside these sense-data

[1] *Ab. K.*, ix, *vidyamānaṃ dravyam*; Yaçom. adds *svalakṣaṇato vidyamānaṃ dravyam.* Cf. *Soul Theory*, p. 943.

[2] *Svalakṣaṇa-dhāraṇād dharmaḥ*, Yaçom. ad *Ab. K.*, i, 3.

there is absolutely nothing the name could be applied to.[1] The same principle is applied to the mental sphere ; there is no spiritual substance apart from mental elements, or faculties, that are conceived as subtle realities or substances *sui generis*, very much on the same pattern as the elements of matter.[2] There is no soul apart from feelings, ideas, volitions, etc.[3] Therefore an element technically means " non-self ".[4]

[1] *Pṛthivī gandhavatīty ukte rūpa-gandha-rasa-sparçebhyo nānyā darçayitum çakyate*, Yaçom. ad *Ab. K.*, ix ; cf. *Soul Theory*, p. 742.

[2] In his *History of Indian Philosophy* (Cambridge, 1922), p. 244, Professor S Dasgupta maintains that in Sānkhya philosophy there is likewise no separate existence of qualities (i.e. no inherence of qualities in a substance). This is based (as the learned author informs me in a letter) on *Vyāsa*, iii, 12 (*sāpekṣiko dharma-dharmi-bhāvaḥ*) and Vācaspati's comment. There are other passages suggestive of a similar idea, e.g. *dharmi-svarūpa-mātro hi dharmaḥ* (ibid., iii, 13). But it is added *dharmi-vikriyaiva eṣā dharma-dvārā prapañcyate*. In Buddhism there cannot be any change of *dharmin*, since everything is new at every moment. Besides it must not be forgotten that Vyāsa, as will be shown later, was strongly influenced by the Abhidharmists. If Professor S. Dasgupta's view that the ultimate entities in Sānkhya were called *guṇas*, probably to suggest that they are the entities which by their various modifications manifest themselves as *guṇas* or qualities, is accepted, this would constitute a very strong analogy between the Sānkhya *guṇas* and the Buddhist *dharmas*. In his *Vijñānamātra-siddhi* Vasubandhu applies the term *dharma* to the *tattvas* of the Sānkhyas (O. Rosenberg).

[3] It is a matter of surprise how long it has taken European science to realize this doctrine, which is so clearly stated in numberless passages of Buddhist writ, and in one of them even in terms very nearly approaching to Hume's statement (*Saṃyutta*, iii, 46) : " all Brahmanas or Çramanas who attentively consider the soul, which so variously has been described to them, find either the five groups of phenomena (physical, feelings, ideas, volitions, or pure sensation) or one of them," etc. The stumbling-block has always been the supposed theory of transmigration of souls and its " glaring " contradiction with the denial of soul. Buddhism always had two languages, one for the learned (*nītārtha*) and one for the simple (*neyārtha*).

[4] *Ab. K.*, ix, cf. *Soul Theory*, p. 840, where it is stated that *anātma* is synonymous with 5 *skandhas*, 12 *āyatanas*, and 18 *dhātus*, i.e. with all *dharmas* ; a single *dharma* is likewise synonymous with *niḥsattva*. It is, therefore, misleading to translate Buddhaghoṣa's interpretation of *dharma* = *nissatta, nijjīva*, as meaning " inanimate thing ", as Mrs. and Prof. Geiger have done, op. cit., p. 4 (Unbelebtes Ding, Sache). Since consciousness itself and all mental phenomena and even Nirvāṇa are *dharmas*, Buddhaghoṣa could not have meant that they are " inanimate things " in the ordinary sense of the word. The compound *nissatta* must be explained either as a *madhyama-pada-lopī—nirgataḥ sattvaḥ*, or as a *bahuvrīhi—nirgataḥ sattvo yasmāt*.

IX. Pratītya-samutpāda (Causality)

Although the separate elements (*dharmas*) are not connected with one another, either by a pervading stuff in space or by duration in time, there is, nevertheless, a connexion between them; their manifestations in time, as well as in space, are subject to definite laws, the laws of causation. These laws bear the general name *pratītya-samutpāda*. We have seen that the connotation of the word *dharma* implies the meaning of elements operating together with others. This concerted life of the elements (*saṃskṛtatva*) is but another name for the laws of causation—the combined origination (*sam-utpāda*) of some elements with regard (*pratītya*) to other elements.[1] Thus it is that the fundamental idea of Buddhism—*the conception of a plurality of separate elements*—includes the idea of the *most strict causality* controlling their operation in the world-process. The "theory of elements"—the *dharma-sanketa*, says Vasubandhu, means that "if something appears, such and such result will follow"—*asmin sati idaṃ bhavati.*[2]

The most popular form of the laws of causation is represented by the theory of the twelve consecutive stages in the ever revolving stream of life from birth to death; it is, so to say, the vertical line of causation, while other relations represent the horizontal.[3]

[1] Yaçom. ad *Ab. K.*, ii, 46: *saṃskṛtatvam pratītya-samutpannatvam iti paryāyāv etau; sametya saṃbhūya pratyayaiḥ kṛtaṃ saṃskṛtam; taṃ taṃ pratyayam pratītya samutpannam, pratītya-samutpannam iti.*

[2] *Ab. K.*, iii, 18 and 28, cf. also ii, 47, and ii, 50.

[3] The interpretation of this formula has been the crux of European scholars, while in Buddhist countries, as Professor O. Rosenberg certifies, it is supposed to be very plain and accessible to the simplest understanding. The right explanation, in the light of the *dharma* theory, will be found in O. Rosenberg's *Problems*, chap. xvi. The stumbling-block to every explanation came from the supposition that the formula was meant to represent some evolution in which one member was producing the other; it was then impossible to deduce e.g. *nāma-rūpa* from *vijñāna*, unless the latter be taken in the sense of the *buddhi* of the Sāṅkhyas. In reality, as soon as the first moment of life (*vijñāna*—third *nidāna*) appears, all the eighteen *dhātus* are already present, according to the principle "there is no *citta* without *caitta*, and no *bhūta* without *bhautika*". On *vijñāna* as the first moment in the life of the embryo cf. *Ab. K.*, i, 35, Tibetan, p. 62, 6, and i, 22, Tibetan, p. 47, 18, and also Mrs. C. Rhys Davids, *B. Psych.*, p. 25. The number of *tattvas* in an embryo, according to Sāṅkhya, is likewise

In the popular literature of the Sūtras the term *pratītya-samutpāda* is almost exclusively applied to this formula of the "wheel of life", although the general meaning of it must have been present to the mind of all Buddhists. It is implied in the division of *dharmas* into *āyatanas,* which is founded on the theory that knowledge arises (*samutpadyate*) when conditioned (*pratītya*) by an object and a receptive faculty. "All *abhi-dharma* is but an interpretation of the sūtras" the current says definition. Therefore the general meaning of the idea of "interconnected origination of elements" may have appeared in the *abhidharma* by a sort of generalization founded on actual conceptions that are to be found in the sūtras in a somewhat different form. This question is directly asked by Vasubandhu. "Why is it," says he, "that the twelve members of interconnected origination of the elements are differently treated in the Scripture and in the Exegesis? e.g. it is stated in the latter that the interconnected origination of elements (*pratītya-samutpāda*) is a term equivalent to all the active elements (*saṃskṛta-dharma*)?" And he answers: "Because in the sūtras this relation is treated intentionally (in a popular way, with reference to the development of an individual's life), whereas the exegetical works explain its essence (in regard of all elements in general)."[1]

Some of the causal relationships have already been mentioned. Thus the relation of simultaneity (*sahabhū*)

eighteen, though there is difference in counting. According to Caraka (*çarīrasthāna*, iv) the sperm-cell of the father contains minute particles of all the organs. Consequently *vijñāna*, as the third member in the "wheel of life", is a *technical term* indicating the first moment of a new life arising out of pre-natal forces (*avidyā, saṃskāra*). The next seven members mark the stages of the development of the embryo into a child, youth, and grown-up man. The *tṛṣṇā*-stage corresponds to sexual maturity, when new *karma* begins to be formed. The two last members refer briefly to future life. The idea that all elements are present through the whole process, the difference being only in the relative "prominence" (*utkarṣas tv abhivyañjakaḥ*, cf. Suçruta, *Sūtrasthāna*, xii) of one element over the others, points out to Sānkhya habits of thought, where everything was considered immutable, always existing (*sarvaṃ nityam*), all things entering in one another (*sarvaṃ sarvātmakam*), the difference being only a passing manifestation of some element, while the others continued to assist in a latent state.

[1] *Ab. K.*, iii, 25. Cf. O. Rosenberg, *Problems*, p. 223.

ties together the four fundamental and the secondary elements of matter—*bhūta* and *bhautika*. The same relation applies to the simultaneous origination of consciousness and mental phenomena (*citta* and *caitta*). But for the vice versa conjunction—one would be tempted to say "inherence" if it was not so grave a mistake against the fundamental principle of Buddhism—of the mental elements with pure consciousness (*citta*), a specific, more intimate, association was imagined. Evidently there was a feeling that the various mental facts were more closely united with consciousness than the atoms of matter with one another. This fact received the name of *samprayoga*, i.e. a thorough and intensive union, and it was explained as *anuparivartana*, i.e. a following and enveloping of consciousness by concomitant mental phenomena of the secondary mental elements (*caitta*). It must not be imagined that this close connexion of consciousness with other mental elements means any unity between them, allowing only a logical distinction for purposes of analysis, as in modern psychologies. A Buddhist element is always a separate entity, it is neither "compound" nor "phenomenon", but an element (*dharma*). The close connexion, "envelopment" of consciousness by other mental elements only means that they are its satellites, they appear and disappear together, they are produced by the same causes, and have the same moral aspect.[1] Ten such satellites are the minimum number to accompany consciousness (*citta*) at every moment; a feeling, an idea, a volition, some attention, some understanding (*mati* = *prajñā*), some concentration (*samādhi*) etc., are always present in every conscious moment.[2] They are

[1] *Ab. K.*, ii, 52, reckons ten different ties of the "satellites" with *citta*. The Theravāda seems to reckon only four, cf. *Asl.*, p. 42: *ekuppādādīnaṃ vasena sampayogattho vutto.*

[2] The number is then increased by the four *saṃskṛta-lakṣaṇas* of each element, and by the four *lakṣaṇas* and four *anulakṣaṇas* of *citta* itself, thus making fifty-eight satellites the minimum number to unite in every single *kṣaṇa* with *citta*, the fifty-ninth (*Ab. K.*, ii, 52).

conjoined, but conjoined by the law of "satellites" (*samprayoga*).[1]

The Sarvāstivādin school reckons in all six different causal relations, but in these details the schools varied a great deal, and they evidently represent a later development of the original idea. The detailed account given in the *Abhidharma-koça* represents the doctrine in its final form which it received in the *abhidharma* of the Sarvāstivādins.

X. Karma

One of the most illuminating features of Buddhist philosophy is its deep research into the phenomenon of moral causation. All Indian systems contain an appeal to the "unknown" (*adṛṣṭa, apūrva*) as a transcendental cause which has to be posited in explaining the origin and the ultimate goal of life. The Buddhists distinguish between (1) causation among elements of dead matter, where the law of homogeneity (*sabhāga-hetu*) between cause and result reigns, (2) causation in the organic world, where we have the phenomenon of growth (*upacaya*), and (3) causation in the animate world, where the operation of moral causation (*vipāka-hetu*) is superimposed upon the natural. The elements constituting the stream of our present life are conditioned, in addition to the natural course of events, by the mysterious efficiency of past elements or deeds, if the latter have possessed a moral character of some force or prominence. The indifferent activities of everyday life have no such efficiency. But a prominent deed, whether good or bad, will affect the whole stream and may carry its result either at an early or very remote date. The resulting event (*vipāka-phala*) is always indifferent (*avyākṛta*) in the

[1] The figurative words of Buddhaghoṣa (quoted by Mrs. Rhys Davids, *B. Psych.*, p. 54) are apparently intended to describe this kind of union. That *vijñāna* is the most general mental element is admitted by all Buddhists; but that it "includes and involves" other elements, let alone aggregates, has never been admitted in *abhidharma*—it would be pure *vijñāna-vāda*. The *samprayoga* connexion is known to Buddhaghoṣa; cf. *Asl.*, p. 42. The *Ab. K.*, i, 35, Tibetan, p. 62, 9, argues that, if the mental phenomena were not different from *citta*, they would not have been called *caitta*.

moral sense, because it is a natural outflow of a previous cause, and is supposed not to be produced voluntarily. This moral law is also called *karma.*

The influence of *karma* is not in the Buddhist outlook so overwhelming, controlling the whole universe, as it is in other non-Buddhist systems, and as it also becomes, under the name of *vāsanā,* in the later idealistic systems of Buddhism also. In *abhidharma* it is one of the forces controlling the world-process : it is the chief force so far as it controls its gradual progress towards Final Deliverance. Its operation is subject to the following conditions. Every fact produced by the "maturing influence" (*vipāka*) of moral or intellectual antecedents (*karma*) necessarily belongs to animate life (*sattvākhyaḥ*), but is by itself morally indifferent (*avyākṛto dharmaḥ*). It is indifferent because it is a natural outcome of antecedents, it always arrives involuntarily, automatically. If something is produced voluntarily, it may become the starting-point of a new development. When it has an outspoken strong moral character, whether good or bad, it becomes *karma,* and will have corresponding consequences which, again, will appear automatically, since they are fully foreshadowed by their antecedent and are not voluntary acts. This explains the definition of *Karma,* as given by Vasubandhu : *Karma* is will (*cetanā*) and voluntary action (*cetayitvā karaṇam*).[1] Exactly the same definition is found in the Pali canon, and evidently was current in Buddhism from the beginning.[2]

When a new life is produced, its component elements, i.e. the eighteen classes (*dhātus*) of elements, are present, although in an undeveloped condition. The first moment of the new life is conventionally called *vijñāna.* It constitutes the third member (*nidāna*) of the ever revolving "wheel of life". Its antecedents are *karma,* i.e. the good or bad instincts sticking to it from the beginning. In the formula of the "wheel of life" this member appears under the name of *saṃskāra,* i.e.

[1] *Ab. K.*, iv, 1 ff.

[2] *Aṅguttara*, vol. iv, 415.

pre-natal forces. Another, more general, antecedent is *avidyā*, the first member of the wheel, representing the defiling influence (*kleça*) of ignorance and other vices, the absence of discriminating knowledge (*prajñā*). Among the components (*dhātu*) of the new life ten represent matter. They are atomic. The atoms are compound atoms, they contain the usual eight components with addition of particles of sensibility-stuff (*rūpa-prasāda*) or "organic" stuff (= *indriya*). The "tangibility"-stuff (*kāyendriya*) pervades the whole body. In some parts of the body, e.g. in the organ of vision, the atoms have a still more complicated structure. But not only does matter consist of compound atoms, it consists of momentary appearances of atoms. In dead, inorganic matter one moment follows the other, obeying solely the law of uniformity or homogeneous production (*sabhāgaja*). The next moment follows automatically (*niṣyanda*) on the former one. There is neither growth nor decay. This uniform course would represent the Buddhist counterpart of what we might call eternity of matter. Although the same matter is also present in the organic body, nevertheless the term "uniform course" (*sabhāga-hetu*) cannot be applied to it in that condition. It is reserved for those cases where there are no other causes in addition to the uniform sequence of moments constituting inorganic matter. When other processes—the process of growth (*upacaya*), the influence of intellectual and moral causes (*vipāka*)—are superimposed upon the uniform course of the existence of matter, when it becomes organic and living, the consecution of its moments receives other names (*upacayaja*, *vipākaja*). The pure "uniformity-relation" between consecutive moments—the *sabhāga-niṣyanda*-relation —obtains only in the realm of inorganic, dead matter. When the atoms of organic matter have assembled, the phenomenon of growth (*upacaya*) becomes the controlling principle of development, the atoms increase in number. This process of growth is supported by favourable circumstances: good food (*anna-viçeṣa*), quiet sleep (*svapna-viçeṣa*), physical tidiness (*saṃskāra-viçeṣa*), and careful behaviour (*samādhi-viçeṣa*). But this growth is not the only factor which controls the development of living bodies. The influence of what we may term heredity steps in, and is superimposed upon the natural process of growth. This is the influence of *karma*, the maturing (*vipāka*) influence of moral antecedents. When the organs of the body are being formed, or are developing, this influence conditions their final constitution. The question is then raised, what is the mutual relation of these two different agencies, natural development and heredity? The answer is that the first process constitutes the "vanguard", or a rampart, under the protection of which the second, the *vipāka*, may safely operate.[1] It is not quite easy to realize what such an answer may exactly mean. At any rate, it suggests a more subtle, spiritual, or semi-spiritual character of the second force. *Karma* is not quite physical (*paudgalika*) with the Buddhists, as it is with the Jains, but it seems to be semi-physical, since it interferes in the disposition of atoms along with the principle of growth that accumulates them.

A very interesting illustration of the meaning of these Buddhist conceptions about heredity, retribution, etc.—all facts falling under the head of *karma-vipāka*—is given by the following scholastic question. Voice is always produced voluntarily, consequently it cannot be the product of moral antecedents, of *karma*. It is not *vipākaja*, for all the facts of heredity are produced automatically (*niṣyanda*). But we know that the Great Man (*mahāpuruṣa*), i.e. a Buddha, has a captivating, melodious voice, a noble elocution. It is one of the characteristic gifts of a Buddha, and is due, like all his sublime qualities, to heredity, i.e. to a long course of moral progress running through generations. Therefore his extraordinary voice and elocution must likewise be a consequence of his moral antecedents (*vipākaja*). The puzzle is solved by

[1] *Ab. K.*, i, 37, and Yaçom.—*upacaya-santāno vipāka-santānasya parivāra-avasthānenaiva ārakṣā.*

assuming a double causality. The configuration of atoms in his organs of speech was influenced by heredity, i.e. moral causes (*vipākaja*), but his actual speech is a voluntary, not an automatical act, and therefore could not be interpreted as a direct product of his sublime nature, or the result of his former achievements.[1]

The elements of moral defilement (*kleça*) are always present in a life (*saṃtāna*), in a latent or patent condition. When latent they have the form of "residues" (*anuçaya*), they stick to the other elements, pollute them, bring them into commotion and prevent their coming down to rest. This influence of the disquieting elements in life is termed "general cause" (*sarvatraga-hetu*) because it affects the whole of the stream of life (*santāna*), all its elements become soiled. The primary cause of this unhappy condition is "illusion" (*avidyā*), the first, fundamental member in the wheel of life. It continues to exist and exhibit its influence as long as the "wheel" turns, and is gradually neutralized and finally stopped by an antidote in the form of transcending wisdom (*prajñā amalā*). Some details about this process will be given later on when dealing with the "unrest" of the elements. This process of gradual extinction of the *kleças* and the consequent purification of life is the ultimate aim of the Buddhist doctrine. For the sake of it the analysis of life into elements, the research into their functions and connexions was undertaken: *sankleça-vyavadānikam idaṃ çāstram*—this doctrine is a doctrine about defilement and purification, or, more exactly, about the commotion and final appeasement of life.[2]

Although emphatically banned from the dwelling of Buddhist philosophy and replaced by the laws of interconnexion, the conceptions of substance and quality seem to have found a back-door through which partly to

[1] *Ab. K.*, i, 37, Tib. text, pp. 65 ff.

[2] The second part of the second *Koça-sthāna* contains an exposition of the *hetu-pratyaya* theory. Cf. also *Ab. K.*, i, 35–6, Tibetan text, pp. 64 ff.

re-enter in their usual position. For the division of the elements of matter into primary and secondary (*bhūta* and *bhautika*) and of the mental elements into fundamental and derivative (*citta* and *caitta*) approaches very nearly the relation of substance and quality. The secondary are supported (*āçrita*) [1] by the primary, and this connexion is inseparable; the one cannot appear without the other. In the Buddhist interpretation they are, nevertheless, separate elements although linked together by the laws of causation. A special relation of simultaneous or reciprocal causation (*sahabhū*) is then imagined to save the situation. In theory the one element is as much the cause of the other as the latter is the cause of the former.[2] The mental phenomena are not included in consciousness (*citta*), but are standing by it, mutually they are enveloping (*anuparivartante*) it, but, nevertheless, they are separate elements.[3] Notwithstanding these efforts to maintain their equal rights, we see that the attempt has not been successful, since there is a primary and secondary position; the secondary is spoken of as supported by the primary, and their connexion is inseparable. It is presumably for this reason that Buddhadeva, one of the celebrities of the Sautrāntika school, revolted against such inequality of treatment, and denied the difference between primary and secondary elements; he maintained that all were equally primary (*bhūta* and not *bhautika*).[4] But this stricture had no success; it was disposed of by reference to the Scriptures and by pointing, as it would seem,

[1] The derived elements of matter are called *upādāya-rūpa*, i.e. *bhūtāni upādāya*; cf. the discussion under *Ab. K.*, i, 35.

[2] Ibid., ii, 51.

[3] It is curious that the *citta* is related to *caitta* by the *sahabhū* relation, which is defined as mutual causality, one member being the cause of the other as much as the latter is the cause of the former. Nevertheless, the *caittas* stand to *citta* in another relation, called *samprayoga*. They "envelop" the *citta*, but do not enter into it, for this would mean "inherence", which is prohibited. Through the cobweb of these devices one can clearly watch the apparition of the ghost of the Soul, which it has cost so much effort to ban.

[4] Ibid., i, 35.

to the prominence of the tactile sense-data; the general manifestations (*lakṣaṇa*) of matter—repulsion, attraction, heat, and motion—are all tactile phenomena, and they are general,[1] whereas colour, etc., can be apprehended by vision alone. Moreover, the translucent matter of the sense organs could not exist (i.e. appear) without being backed by some more consistent forces.[2]

XI. Impermanence of the Elements

The elements of existence are momentary appearances, momentary flashings into the phenomenal world out of an unknown source. Just as they are disconnected, so to say, in breadth, not being linked together by any pervading substance, just so are they disconnected in depth or in duration, since they last only one single moment (*kṣaṇa*). They disappear as soon as they appear, in order to be followed the next moment by another momentary existence. Thus a moment becomes a synonym of an element (*dharma*), two moments are two different elements. An element becomes something like a point in time-space. The Sarvāstivādin school makes an attempt mathematically to determine the duration of a moment.[3] It, nevertheless, admittedly represents the smallest particle of time imaginable. Such computations of the size of the atom and of the duration of a moment are evidently mere attempts to seize the infinitesimal. The idea that two moments make two different elements

[1] Caraka (*Çarīrasthāna*, chap. i) likewise points out that the *lakṣaṇas* of his five *bhūtas* are tactile phenomena—*sparç-endriya-gocaram.*

[2] Buddhadeva in his turn quotes the *Garbhāvakrānti-sūtra* (not to be traced in the Pali canon) and a passage stating that at the conception moment of Buddha (i.e. the third *nidāna*, technically called *vijñāna*) the embryo was *ṣaḍdhātuka*, i.e. consisting of six elements, *vijñāna*, four *mahābhūtas*, and *ākāça*: the *bhautikas* are not mentioned. But it is answered that the *mahābhūtas* are alone mentioned, since *bhūta* represents the *bhautikas* as well, and *vijñāna* is here equivalent to *citta* and *caitta* (*Ab. K.*, i, 35, Tibetan text, p. 62, 6 ff.). Suçruta (*Sūtra-sthāna*, xii) has the same view as Buddhadeva. He likewise shares the view that the prominence, *utkarṣa*, not the quantity, of one kind of atoms, determines the class of the compound.

[3] *Ab. K.*, iii, 15; cf. S. Z. Aung, *Compendium*, p. 25.

remains. Consequently, the elements do not change, but disappear, the world becomes a cinema. Disappearance is the very essence of existence; what does not disappear does not exist.[1] A cause for the Buddhists was not a real cause but a preceding moment, which likewise arose out of nothing in order to disappear into nothing.

It is at present impossible to determine the epoch when this theory was definitely framed. Some of the oldest schools, at any rate, expressed it very clearly.[2] They maintained that mountains, trees, the elements of matter, all elements in general, were momentary apparitions, like moments of thought. The schools differed on this point, and the complete logical demonstration was constructed, probably, at the time when logic had taken the place of *abhidharma*.[3] But it is easy to realize that, given the fundamental Buddhist idea of the plurality and separateness (*pṛthaktva*) of their elements, this idea, worked out with the characteristic Indian intrepidity in philosophical construction, must have been carried to its logical consequence, i.e. the assuming of no duration, since there was no stuff that could possess duration.

[1] Thus existence becomes synonymous with non-existence, since every fact disappears at the same moment when it appears. This is the Indian way of expressing the idea developed by H. Bergson, *Creative Evolution*, p. 2: "the truth is that we change without ceasing, and that the state itself is nothing but change." The conclusion of Bergson is to the indivisibility of duration, whereas the Buddhists stick to the separate moments and make them appear out of nothing—*asata utpādaḥ*—and again disappear into nothing—*niranvaya-vināçaḥ*; cf. *Nyāyabinduṭ.*, p. 68. *Vedānta-sūtra*, ii, 2, 6, and *Sānkhya-sūtra*, i, 44–5, accuse the Buddhists of converting existence into non-existence.

[2] *Kathāvatthu*, xxii, 8: *eka-citta-khaṇikā sabbe dhammā.*

[3] The ancient term seems to have been *anitya*, which is accepted by all schools. It was replaced in the sequel by *kṣaṇika*. This may reflect some change in the definiteness of the view. The logical argument is that every moment being a different determination, must be a separate entity: *viruddha-dharma-saṃsargād dhy anyad vastu*, cf. *Nyāyabinduṭīkā*, p. 5 (*Bibl. Ind.*). By the conversion of the proposition *yat sat tat kṣaṇikam* it was proved that, if something did not disappear, it did not exist. The doctrine is fully expounded in Ratnakīrti's *Kṣaṇabhangasiddhi* (Six Buddhist tracts, *Bibl. Ind.*), and it is controverted in numerous Brahmanical werks

A consequence of this doctrine was a denial of motion. A really existing object, i.e. an element, cannot move, because it disappears as soon as it appears, there is no time for it to move. This does not contradict the circumstance that one of the general characteristics of matter, the fourth *mahābhūta*, is motion. Every motion is resolved in a series of separate apparitions, or flashings, arising in contiguity to one another.[1] Motion of physical objects, as explained in the *abhidharma*, gave the best support to the consideration of dead matter as a series of evanescent flashings. The phenomen of acceleration of falling bodies is explained by a difference in the intensity of the element weight or motion (*īraṇa*) at every moment of its downward course, since the object at every moment is differently composed.[2] An element is thus comparable to a fire, it consists of a series of separate flashings following one another, every moment representing a new fire.

The Sarvāstivādins construe the theory of the momentary character of the elements in the following manner.[3] Every element appearing in phenomenal life is affected simultaneously by four different forces (*saṃskāras*), the forces of origination (*utpāda*), decay (*jarā*), maintenance (*sthiti*), destruction (*anityatā*).[4] These forces affect every element at every moment of its existence, they are the most universal forces, the characteristic feature or the manifesting forces of phenomenal existence (*saṃskṛta-lakṣaṇāni*). The elements affected by them are called the manifested elements (*saṃskṛta-dharma*). Unaffected by them are only the three

[1] *Ab. K.*, iv, 2, *na gatir, nāçāt*: it is not *kriyā*, but *nirantara-utpāda*, see below, under Theory of Cognition, p. 60.

[2] *Ab. K.*, ii, 46. The Vaiçeṣika admit one indivisible *saṃskāra* till the cessation of a motion. This would correspond to Bergson's idea of the indivisibility of motion. The Naiyāyikas, on the contrary, admit as many *saṃskāras* as there are momentary *kriyās*.

[3] It is expounded with all details of the issue between Sautrāntikas and Sarvāstivādins by Vasubandhu in *Ab. K.*, ii, 46. Professor L. de la Vallée Poussin has kindly communicated to me his French translation of this important text, which I compared with my own English translation.

[4] Sometimes reduced to three—birth, subsistence, and decay.

elements of eternal unchanging existence (*asaṃskṛta-dharma*). The term *saṃskṛta* is therefore synonymous with *kṣaṇika*, i.e. impermanent or momentary.[1]

According to the laws of interconnexion between elements, these four forces always appear together and simultaneously. They are *sahabhū*.[2] Being elements themselves, they are in need of secondary forces (*upalakṣaṇa*) in order to display their efficiency. The realistic tendency of the Sarvāstivādins, if there was any, consisted in constructing some realities corresponding to our ideas or habits of speech. This tendency they shared with the Nyāya-Vaiçeṣika system. Just as the latter had a quality of conjunction (*saṃyoga*) as something real, additional to the things which were joining, just so the Sarvāstivādins had their origination, decay, existence, and destruction in addition to the elements originating and disappearing at the same moment. They insisted that these four forces, and the secondary potencies influencing them in their turn, were realities (*dravyataḥ santi*). Against this idea of an element which was simultaneously originating, existing, and disappearing, the very natural objection was raised by all the other Buddhist and non-Buddhist schools that production and destruction could not be simultaneous. On the other hand, it was impossible to allow an element more than one single moment's duration, since two moments constituted two elements. The Sarvāstivādins met the objection by pointing to the difference between an element in itself, its real nature (*svabhāva*) and its efficiency-moment, its function, or manifestation (*kāritva, lakṣaṇa*). The elements or forces may be opposed to one another, yet their effect may result in some single real fact, as e.g., supposing three assassins have resolved together to kill a man hiding in some

[1] The translation of *saṃskṛta-dharma* as "compound" is a *contradictio in adjecto*. A *dharma* is never compound, it is always simple. Wherever there is composition there are several *dharmas*.

[2] Just as the *citta* never appears without simultaneously being accompanied by *caitta-dharmas*, or the four *mahābhūtas* appearing simultaneously with the *bhautikas*.

dark recess, one of them (*utpāda*) pulls him out of his hiding-place (the future), the other seizes him, the third stabs him, all acting simultaneously. The victim (*dharma*) appears only to disappear. The reality moment is the moment of action, of its being achieved. "We call a moment," the Sarvāstivādins maintain, "the point when an action is fully achieved."[1] We have here the germ of the later idea that this moment is something transcendental, something that cannot be expressed in a discursive thought.[2] The moment was then raised to the position of the "thing in itself",[3] the transcendental foundation of reality; indeed, the absolute reality itself[4]—a conception which had great importance in the development of later Indian philosophy.[5]

The Sautrāntika school takes a more simple and reasonable view of the question. They deny the reality of the four manifestation-forces of production, decay, etc.[6] The corresponding notions of production, destruction, etc., refer, not to single moments, but to series of them (*santāna*).[7] Even if applied to one moment these notions do not imply the existence of corresponding realities, they are mere names for the fact that a momentary entity appears and disappears.[7] This entity itself appears and disappears, there is no need of supplementary forces for this. Consequent on that, a further very important divergence between the two schools arises. As stated above, the Sarvāstivādins maintain that all elements

[1] *Kriyā-parisamāpti-lakṣaṇa eṣo naḥ kṣaṇaḥ*, *Ab. K.*, ii, 46; cf. Nyāyabinduṭīkā, p. 13 (*Bibl. Ind.*): *kṣanike vastuni . . . eka-kriyā-kāritvena sahakārī gṛhyate.*

[2] *Kṣaṇasya (jñānena) prāpayitum açakyatvāt* (ibid., p. 16).

[3] *Svalakṣaṇa*, ibid.

[4] *Paramārtha-sat*, ibid.

[5] Dharmakīrti identified the moment with pure sensation, where subject and object coalesce, and the Vedantins deemed that we have in this moment a direct perception of *brahma*. The Indian astronomers and mathematicians knew the differential conception of instantaneous motion of a planet, *tātkālikī gatiḥ*, a motion constant during an infinitesimally small interval; cf. B. Seal, *Positive Sciences*, p. 77.

[6] *Dravyato na santi*, cf. *Ab. K.*, ii, 46.

[7] Ibid

exist on two different planes, the real essence of the element (*dharma-svabhāva*) and its momentary manifestation (*dharma-lakṣaṇa*). The first exists always, in past, present, and future. It is not eternal (*nitya*) because eternality means absence of change, but it represents the potential appearances of the element into phenomenal existence, and its past appearances as well. This potentiality is existing for ever (*sarvadā asti*). Even in the suppressed state of Nirvāṇa, when all life is extinct, these elements are supposed to represent some entity, although its manifestation-power has been suppressed for ever. The future potential elements are, indeed, divided in this school into two different sets, those that will appear (*utpatti-dharma*) and those that are suppressed and never will appear (*anutpatti-dharma*). Since the moment (*kṣaṇa*) is not something different from the element (*dharma*), time in general is not different from the elements taken collectively, as far as they have not lost their capacity of appearing in phenomenal life. In fact, " the times " is one of the synonyms used to designate collectively the elements appearing in ordinary life.[1] But the term " time " (*kāla*), implying the reality of one time, is carefully avoided; it is replaced by the term " transition " (*adhvan*). When the Sarvāstivādin maintains that " everything exists ", it means that all elements exist, and the emphasis which is put on the reality of elements refers to the conception that their past as well as their future transition represents something real. From this fundamental tenet the school derives its name. Since the conception of an element answers rather to our conception of a subtle force than of a substance, the reality, i.e. effectiveness, of the past is not so absurd as it otherwise would appear. The Sautrāntikas denied the reality of the past and the future in the direct sense, they admitted the reality only of the present. The future, they contended, was not real before becoming present, and the past was not real after having been

[1] *upādāna-skandha*, cf. *Ab. K.*, i, 7, Tibetan text, p. 12, 6.

present.[1] They did not deny the influence of past facts upon present and remote future ones, but they explained it by a gradual change in an uninterrupted sequence of moments, this sequence having a starting-point in a conspicuous or strong impingeing fact; it was for them one of the laws of interconnexion between separate elements.[2]

There was another school which occupied an intermediate position between the Sautrāntikas and Sarvāstivādins; it maintained the reality of the present facts and of that part of the past ones which had not already lost their influence, but the reality of the future ones and of that part of the past ones which had ceased to exhibit any influence it denied. Vasubandhu calls this school the Vibhajyavādins, or Distinguishing School.[3] The whole argument between the rival schools is presented by Vasubandhu with every detail in his usual masterly manner and need not be repeated here.[4]

XII. Impermanence in Sānkhya-Yoga

The deprecation of "change and decay" and its contrast with something that "changes not" is a popular theme with many religions and philosophies. The merit of having worked it out up to the remotest logical consequences appertains to Buddhism. It appears that in this work the Buddhists were assisted by the parallel work of Brahmanical philosophers of the Sānkhya-Yoga school. The starting-point of the latter was just the reverse of the Buddhistic one. They maintained a unity of existence, cause and effect were one in essence. But a corollary of the

[1] *Ab. K.*, v, 24 ff., cf. Appendix I.

[2] *Ab. K.*, ix, cf. *Soul Theory*, p. 949.

[3] In the *Kathāvatthu*, i, 8, such opinions are ascribed to the Kāçyapīyas. These also admitted the reality of that part of the future which was foreshadowed or fixed by the past or present. Hiuen Thsang states in his Commentary that the Kāçyapīyas are here meant under the name of Vibhajyavādins (McGovern). The Theravādins seem to have shared the same opinions as the Sautrāntikas. The explanation of *vibhajya-vāda* as orthodoxy or analytic school because Buddha himself was *vibhajya-vādin* (cf. *Kathāvatthu*, introduction) seems to be unknown to Vasubandhu.

[4] Cf. translation in Appendix I.

unity of substance (*satkārya-vāda*) was the constant change of its manifestations; this change was also conceived as momentary (*pratikṣaṇa-pariṇāma*). The moment is here defined as the infinitesimally small measure of time, just as the atom is the smallest imaginable fraction of matter.[1] Two moments cannot coalesce,[2] therefore there is no real duration, no time outside the moment.[3] Time is an idea without reality, an empty construction of the mind.[4] The only reality is the momentary thing. The past and the future are not real directly, but, since the present cannot exist without a past, the latter is inherent in the fact of change.[5] "Therefore," says Vyāsa, "the whole universe is included in one single moment, all the real units of change you may imagine[6] are merged in every single moment."[7] Concluding, Vyāsa admits two kinds of eternity, immutable eternity belonging to the soul and eternity of mutation belonging to matter.[8] The unit of change is termed *dharma*, and it is identified with the moment (*kṣaṇa*) in Yoga as well as in Buddhism. The change of manifestation was called a change of *dharma*[9]; but in the Brahmanical system it is quite natural to make use of this term, since an old and usual meaning of it is "quality", and in the Sānkhya view the changing manifestations are appurtenances of some pervading stuff. It is therefore probable that the technical meaning of this term in Buddhism developed from one of its old meanings, with the difference that, quality being left without any support by the substance, it became an independent quality, or quality in the role of substance. As in the Buddhist system, these manifestations

[1] Vyāsa's *Bhāṣya*, ad iii, 52.
[2] Ibid.
[3] *Kṣaṇa-tatkramayor nāsti vastu-samāhāraḥ*, ibid.
[4] *Vastuçūnyo buddhinirmāṇaḥ*, ibid.
[5] *Pariṇāmānvitaḥ*, ibid.
[6] Ibid., *amī sarve dharmāḥ*.
[7] Ibid., *tatkṣaṇoparuddhāḥ*.
[8] Ibid., iv, 33.
[9] Ibid., iii, 13.

are conceived as forces (*çakti*)[1] and even potential forces (*yogyatāvacchinna*),[2] corresponding to the Buddhist conception of a *saṃskāra*. The difference is that they belong to some substance (*dharmin*). The reality of a "transition-time" (*adhvan*) as distinguished from a "duration-time" (*kāla*) was admitted; the same term—*adhvan*—is used on both sides to express the first of these conceptions.[3]

If we turn to the Sarvāstivādin view, which admitted some transcendental everlasting reality of the elements along with their passing manifestations, the similarity becomes still more striking, and the difference is often restricted to the wording. A *dharma*, says Vyāsa, exists in all the three times.[4] The manifestation (*dharma*) and the manifested (*dharmin*) are quite the same, the manifestation represents only the way in which the manifested appears.[5] The reality of the past and the future is then proved by Patanjali and Vyāsa in almost the same expressions that are used by the Sarvāstivādins,[6] with the difference that there is no mention of separate forces (*saṃskṛtà-lakṣaṇāni*) of production and destruction. When accused of drifting into Sānkhya, the Sarvāstivādins justified themselves by pointing to these momentary forces, which saved the Buddhist principle of detached entities.[7]

The question of the relation between the permanent essence of an element and its manifestation was thoroughly discussed

[1] Ibid., iii, 14.
[2] Ibid.
[3] Ibid., iv, 12.
[4] Ibid., iii, 13.
[5] Ibid.
[6] The Sarvāstivādins argue that the past and the future must exist because we have a knowledge of the past and of the future objects; this knowledge cannot be of non-existence, i.e. of nothing. We find quite the same argument in *Vyāsa-bhāṣya*, ad iv, 12, cf. Appendix I. Stress is laid upon the conception *adhvan* "transition", when the reality of past and present are asserted: *adhva-viçiṣṭatayā sattvaṃ trayāṇām apy aviçiṣṭam* (Vācaspati ad *Vyāsa-bhāṣya*, iv, 12). This reality is inherent in the fact of transition: *ye tu bhūta-bhāvinaḥ kṣaṇās te pariṇāmānvitā vyākhyeyāḥ* (ibid., iii, 52). Otherwise there would be contradiction between iv, 12, and iii, 52, where it is said: *na pūrvottara-kṣaṇāḥ santi*.
[7] Cf. Appendix I.

among Buddhists, and four solutions were suggested. The first belonged to Dharmatrāta[1]: it maintained unity of substance (*dravya*) along with a change in existence (*bhāva*). This was dismissed by simply pointing to the obvious fact that this was Sānkhya and not Buddhism. The second explanation belonged to Ghoṣa; it assumed that elements, although existent in the past, present, and future, changed their aspect (*lakṣaṇa*), or intensity, accordingly as they appeared at different times; just as the passionate love for one woman is only an intensification of a feeling which is alive towards women in general; it does not mean total absence of this feeling in other cases. This explanation was not accepted on the ground that it implied co-existence of the different aspects at the same time. Vasumitra advocated a change of condition (*avasthā*), i.e. of efficiency (*kāritva*) in the present, and non-efficiency in past and future. This view was accepted in the school as the correct one. It was illustrated by the ball of an Indian abacus: being thrown in the hole for units it means one, in the hole for hundreds—hundred, etc. Finally Buddhadeva thought that past, present, and future were contingent (*apekṣā*) upon one another, just as the same woman may be a mother with respect to her child and a daughter with respect to her mother. This was dismissed as leading to a confusion of the times. The passage of the *Vibhāṣā*, where these opinions of four celebrated masters of the Sarvāstivādin and Sautrāntika schools were reported, enjoyed apparently great popularity. Reference is made to it in later Buddhist works,[2] and it evidently was borrowed from the Buddhists by Patanjali and Vyāsa. *Yogasūtra*, iii, 13, aims at giving an explanation of the time variations of one substance; it adopts the suggested explanations not as exclusive of one another, but as subordinate and co-existent. The change of manifestation (*dharma*) is characterized further on as a change

[1] Ibid.

[2] As e.g. in Bhavya's account of the sects; cf. Rockhill's *Life of Buddha*.

of aspect (*lakṣaṇa*) and condition (*avasthā*). The characteristic examples for illustrating the suggested explanations are repeated in Vyāsa's *Bhāṣya* with slight modifications. As though answering the variety of the Buddhist theories, Vyāsa emphatically maintains that the change of quality (*dharma*), aspect (*lakṣaṇa*), and condition (*avasthā*) is but the same fact variously described. "There is, therefore," says he, "only one kind of mutation of matter, though variously described by us . . . The mutations of external aspect (*dharma*) and of time-variation (*lakṣaṇa*) and of intensity (*avasthā*), as here described, do not transcend the substance as such. Hence there is only one kind of mutation which includes all those varieties we have described."[1] Buddhadeva's theory that the time variations are contingent upon one another, which logically leads to the conclusion that essence and manifestation are interchangeable terms, may have influenced the somewhat similar theory of Patanjali and Vyāsa that substance and quality are contingent (*sāpekṣika*) terms.[2]

The doctrine of momentary universal change originated probably in the Sānkhya system. From this doctrine it receives the name of a Theory of Change—*pariṇāma-vāda*, which is only a natural corollary of its fundamental principle of unity between cause and effect (*satkārya-vāda*). It is natural to surmise that early Buddhism has been influenced by it. But in a later period the Sarvāstivādin philosophers unquestionably exercised a considerable influence on the formation of the Sānkhya-Yoga doctrine.[3]

[1] Cf. Professor J. H. Woods' translation in his *Yoga System of Patañjali* (Harvard O.S.), p. 217.

[2] *Vyāsa*, iii, 15.

[3] The points of similarity between the Buddhist system and the Sānkhya-Yoga, especially as presented in the *Yoga-Sūtra* and *Bhāṣya*, are so overwhelmingly numerous that they could not escape the attention of the students of *abhidharma*. Some of them have been occasionally noticed above. The point deserves special treatment. Professor de la Vallée Poussin has kindly communicated to me in MS. a paper prepared by him on the subject. He also informs me that Professor Kimura in Japan has arrived at the same conclusions independently from him.

XIII. Unrest of the Elements

The third salient feature of Buddhist elements is that they represent *duḥkha*, a term which has always been rendered by suffering, sorrow, etc. Sufficient as this interpretation may be for popular literature, it is evident that theoretically something else is meant. Such expressions as "the element of vision (*cakṣuḥ*) is sorrow",[1] "all elements influenced (*sāsrava*, i.e. influenced by desire to live) are sorrow"[2]—an element "colour" might be brought under the head of "sorrow" as well[3]—could not be understood if our usual idea of sorrow was brought in. The idea underlying it is that the elements described above are perpetually in a state of commotion, and the ultimate goal of the world process consists in their gradual appeasement and final extinction. The old Buddhist credo (*ye dharmā hetu-prabhavāḥ*) already expresses the idea very sharply: "the Great Recluse has indicated the (separate) elements, their interconnexion as causes and effects, and their final suppression."

Vasubandhu likewise[4] states that Buddha in his compassion for the troubles of mankind offered them a means of salvation which did not consist of magic or religious boons, but of the knowledge of a method of converting all *utpatti-dharmas* into

[1] *Ab. K.*, i, 19, Tibetan text, p. 31, 5.

[2] Ibid., i, 9, Tibetan text, p. 13, 6.

[3] Because it is entered into the *upādāna-skandhas*, a synonym of which is *duḥkha* and *duḥkha-samudaya* (*Ab. K.*, i, 8, Tibetan text, B.W.). The translation of *ārya-satya* by "Aryan facts" (M. Ting and Mrs. Rhys Davids) is evidently better than the old translation "truth". What is really meant is a distribution of the elements (*dharma*) into four stages, unrest (*duḥkha*) and its cause (*samudaya*), final appeasement (*nirodha*) and its cause (*mārga*), a formula of elements corresponding to every stage. The *sāsrava-dharmas* are the same as *duḥkha* and *samudaya*, the *anāsrava-dharmas* the same as *nirodha* and *mārga*; cf. *Ab. K.*, i, 3. Thus *duḥkha* in this formula does not at all mean "sorrow", but it is a synonym of the seventy-two *dharmas*, or the five *upādāna-skandhas*. Its general meaning is exactly the same as the meaning of the formula *ye dhammā*. This *duḥkha* is *pariṇāma-duḥkha*. Evidently Ledi Sadaw had this conception in view when pointing to the difference between two kinds of *dukkha*; cf. Mrs. Rhys Davids, *B. Psych.*, p. 83. Cf. S. Schayer, *Mahāyānistische Erlösungslehren*, p. 6.

[4] Ad *Ab. K.*, i, 1.

anutpatti-dharmas, i.e. of stopping for ever the commotion created by the operation of the forces active in the process of life.[1] Our conception of a Buddhist element (*dharma*) would not be complete if this connotation of a commotion to be suppressed (*heya*) were not included, along with its non-substantiality and momentary evanescence.

This feature converts the *dharma*-theory into a doctrine of salvation—the chief aim of theoretical as well as practical Buddhism. The doctrine amounts shortly to the following details. From the view-point of a gradual progress towards Final Deliverance all the elements of life may assume two different characters: they either are characterized by a tendency towards life, commotion and turmoil, and then they are called *sāsrava*,[2] i.e. "influenced" by passions; or they are "uninfluenced" (*anāsrava*), i.e. they exhibit the opposite tendency towards reduction of life, appeasement of commotion and even annihilation.[3] The passions (*kleça*), being themselves separate elements, i.e. represented as substantial entities, affect the stream of life (*santāna*) to which they belong. Roughly, the first set of elements (the *sāsrava-dharmas*) correspond to the ordinary man, with all his enjoyments and bothers in life; the second make up the saint (*ārya*), who stands aloof from all interest in life and cares only for Final Deliverance. A thorough knowledge, a discrimination,[4] of all elements of existence is essential for Salvation, since when they are known they can be singled out and gradually suppressed one after the other. The connotation of the term "element" (*dharma*) thus includes three further conceptions: (1) it is something that can be well determined, i.e. distinguished in the complex stream of life as an ultimate

[1] *Ab. K.*, i, 1.

[2] Cf. *Ab. K.*, i, 3. The derivation of the word from the root *sru* is, no doubt, correct, as is proved by the Jaina view of the *karma* matter "flowing" into the body through the pores of the skin.

[3] The eternal *asaṃskṛta* elements are included among the *anāsrava* class (*Ab. K.*, i, 3).

[4] *Ab. K.*, i, 2, *dharma-pravicaya*—a thorough picking out of elements one by one.

reality; (2) this something is in a state of eternal commotion; (3) it is something that must and can be appeased, and brought to an eternal standstill.[1]

A special element received in this connexion extraordinary prominence. It is termed *prajñā*, which may roughly be translated "understanding". It is one of the *città-mahā-bhūmika* elements, i.e. a mental faculty always present, in every conscious moment. In the ordinary plane of existence it is synonymous with *mati* and means simple understanding, the capacity of appreciating something. But it is capable of development and becomes then *prajñā amalā*, "immaculate wisdom," *anāsravā prajñā*, "understanding uninfluenced (by mundane considerations)." Its presence gives the whole stream (*santāna*) a special character, it becomes the central element of the stream, and its satellites—all other elements of the "stream"—feelings, ideas, volitions, become pure.[2] The presence of this element acts as an antidote against other elements that are "unfavourable" (*akuçala*) for progress; they gradually disappear and cannot reappear in the same stream. The first thing to be realized in such a state is the theory of the elements (*dharmatā*), the idea that there is no permanent personality (*pudgala, ātmā*), that the supposed personality really is a congeries of eighteen components (*dhātu*). When the wrong view of an existing personality (*satkāya-dṛṣṭi*) is disposed of, the path that leads to Final Deliverance is entered. Every vicious, or disquieting, "unfavourable" (*akuçala*) element has a special antidote in the agency of wisdom; when suppressed it becomes an *anupatti-dharma*, an element which never will return, a blank is substituted for it; this blank (*nirodha*) is called "cessation through

[1] In the terminology of *abhidharma* "something to be suppressed" means that it is an element (*dharma*); cf. *Ab. K.*, i, 15, Tibetan text, 27, 8. If something is not mentioned among the objects to be suppressed, that means that it is not a *dharma*; cf. *Ab. K.*, ix, *Soul Theory*, p. 844. Something to be "well known, thoroughly known" means likewise that it is a *dharma* (ibid., p. 837).

[2] *Ab. K.*, i, 2, and Yaçom. comment.

wisdom" (*pratisankhyā-nirodha*).[1] But only the initial stages of saintliness can be reached through this so-called *dṛsti-mārga*, i.e. through knowledge a certain amount of *dharmas* has its flashings stopped. The remainder are stopped by mystical concentration, they are *bhāvanā-heya*,[2] i.e. to be suppressed by entering the realms of trance. In all Indian systems the ultimate instrument of salvation is Yoga. This can not only do away with the intellectual and moral elements that are "unfavourable", but can stop the existence or appearance of matter itself. We have seen that matter is reduced in this system to sense-data, which are conceived rather as forces, momentary flashings. Practical observation has shown to the philosophers that when a certain degree of intense concentration is reached the sensations of taste and smell disappear, hence, it is concluded, the objects, the sense-data of odour and taste, have likewise vanished. Founded on this practical observation, a plane of existence has been imagined,[3] where living beings or "streams" (*santāna*) consist only of fourteen instead of eighteen components.[4] In the *Abhidharma-koça* the question is raised, how many elements can be suppressed through knowledge and how many through ecstasy? and it is answered that some mental elements are suppressed by mere knowledge only, namely, the belief in a real personality (*sat-kāya-dṛṣṭi*) and its

[1] *Pratisankhyā* is synonymous with *prajñā amalā*; it is the same as the *prajñā* or *prasankhyāna* in the Sānkhya-Yoga system, an agency destroying the *kleças*. It was probably the original meaning of the word *saṃkhyā*, from which the system received its name. The Buddhist specification in the way of the preposition *prati-* refers to the separateness of the elements, of which every one needs a separate action of wisdom in order to be suppressed; cf. *Ab. K.*, i, 4. The same tendency is probably responsible for the term *prati-mokṣa* instead of *mokṣa*, as *prati-vijñaptiḥ*, cf. above, p. 16; the term *prati-buddha*, on the contrary, is used as a designation of the "Enlightened One", in the Upanisads (cf. H. Oldenberg, *Die Lehere dur Upanishaden*, p. 131), by Jains, Sānkhyas, but not by Buddhists.

[2] *Ab. K.*, i, 20.

[3] *Ab. K.*, *bhāṣya*, ad i, 30, Tibetan text, p. 53, 4, where this explanation is attributed to Çrīlābha, and is, evidently, shared by Vasubandhu himself.

[4] The *dhātus* Nos. 8–7 and 14–15 are in abeyance.

consequences—all the feelings, ideas, and volitions and forces connected—they disappear as soon as the antidote, i.e. the *anātma* = *dharma*-theory, is realized. Other impure elements (*sāsrava*), all the material elements (*dhātus* 1–5 and 7–10), and all sensuous consciousness (*dhātus* 13–17 ; fifteen *dhātus* in all) can be suppressed only by ecstasy.[1] Since matter was conceived as a play of subtle forces, its disappearance in a manner similar to the suppression of passion and wrong views is not so illogical. The purified elements of the saint (*anāsrava-dharma*) could not be suppressed at all, but they likewise disappeared at the time of Nirvāṇa, through absence of new *karma*, i.e. elements of unrest (*duḥkha*), to which the commotion of the world was due. Imagination has constructed whole worlds where these kinds of matter and sensations corresponding to them are absent, they are the worlds of reduced, or purified, matter.[2] They can be entered either by rebirth in them (*utpatti*), or by an effort of concentration (*samāpatti*), an absorption which transports into higher planes of existence not merely Buddhists. Working further on upon the same principle, higher worlds are constructed where the material side—the sense-data—experience further reduction and finally worlds purely spiritual are reached, where every matter, i.e. all sensations and sense-data are absent. Speaking technically, the formula of a living being in these planes of existence will reveal only three component terms (*dhātu*) : consciousness (*mano-dhātu*), mental phenomena and forces (*dharma-dhātu*), and abstract, non-sensuous cognition (*mano-vijñānd-dhātu*).[3] These purely spiritual beings (or, more precisely, formulas of being) have their consciousness and mental phenomena brought to a standstill at some very high planes of transic existence : the unconscious trance (*asanjñi-samāpatti*) and cessation trance (*nirodhā-samāpatti*). But this is, nevertheless,

[1] *Ab. K.*, i, 40.
[2] *Ab. K.*, i, 30, *rūpa-Dhātu*.
[3] *Ab. K.*, i, 31.

not an eternal extinction. At last the absolute stoppage of all the pure *dharmas* of the highest spiritual beings is reached, an eternal blank is substituted for them. This is Nirvāṇa, absolute annihilation of the *saṃskṛta-dharmas*, which is tantamount to the presence of the *asaṃskṛta-dharmas*.

According to the Sarvāstivādins, this quite negative result is, nevertheless, an entity of some kind. They make a difference, as stated above, between the essence and the manifestations of the *dharmas*. At the time of Nirvāṇa the manifestations have ceased for ever, there will be no rebirth, but this essence remains. It is, nevertheless, a kind of entity where there is no consciousness.

Thus the ultimate goal of the world-process, the final result of all purifying, spiritualizing agencies and efforts is a complete extinction of consciousness and all mental processes. The absolute (*nirvāṇa*) is inanimate, even if it is something. It is sometimes, especially in popular literature, characterized as bliss, but this bliss consists in the cessation of unrest (*duḥkha*). Bliss is a feeling, and in the absolute there neither is a feeling, nor conception, nor volition, nor even consciousness. The theory is that consciousness cannot appear alone without its satellites, the phenomena of feeling, volition, etc.,[1] and the last moment in the life of a *bodhisattva*, before merging into the absolute, is also the last moment of consciousness in his continuity of many lives.[2] The appeasement of wrongs and passions is the general ideal of humanity; but this appeasement carried further on and raised to the state of absolute insensibility is a peculiarity of the Hindu ideal. Philosophy has converted that into conceptual formulas, and the result may seem absurd, but "whosoever wishes to be a philosopher must learn not to be frightened by absurdities", says a distinguished modern author.[3] Buddhism was not the only Indian system of philosophy to arrive at

[1] *Ab. K.*, ii.
[2] Ibid., i, 17, Tibetan text, p. 30, 5.
[3] Bertrand Russell, *Problems of Philosophy*, p. 31.

such a result: in the Vaiçeṣika system the liberated soul is as inanimate as a stone (*pāṣāṇavat*), or as ether (*ākāçavat*), because cognition, feeling, etc., are not considered as of its essence, but as an accidental quality produced by special contacts, which cease when final deliverance is reached.[1] The absolute is spiritual only in those systems which accept the doctrine that consciousness is of the essence of the absolute, i.e. the doctrine of self-luminosity (*sva-prakāça*) of knowledge.[2]

XIV. Theory of Cognition

The character of a philosophical system generally comes forth very clearly in its theory of cognition; it enables us to assign it a place among either the realistic systems, maintaining the reality of the outer world, or among the idealistic ones, denying such reality. Among the Indian systems we find every variety of such theories represented. The Nyāya-Vaiçeṣika system favoured a naively realistic view of a series of real contacts—of the object with the sense-organ, of the latter with an internal organ, which in its turn entered into contact with the soul, and thus cognition was produced. The Buddhist idealistic school of Dignāga and Dharmakīrti developed a transcendental theory which exhibited some striking points of similarity with the transcendental theory of Kant. The Sānkhya-Yoga system would explain the origin of knowledge through an assumed assimilation of the mind-stuff to the object through the medium of a sense-organ, compared with the attraction of an object by a magnet.[3] Even later Vedānta, notwithstanding its strictly monistic principle, managed to establish some kind of realistic view about "seizing" the object by the senses.[4] What was, as compared with these views, the conception of earlier Buddhism, that part of Buddhist philosophy which

[1] Cf. references in A. B. Keith's *Indian Logic*, p. 261 n.

[2] Clearly expressed by Dharmakīrti in the celebrated verse: *avibhāgo hi buddyātmā. . .*

[3] *Yoga Sūtra*, i, 4, 7.

[4] *Vedānta-sāra*, 29.

admitted the existence of elements (*dharma*) as ultimate realities, i.e. the Sarvāstivādins and the Sautrāntikas ?

Their explanation of the origin of knowledge was in perfect agreement with their ontology, i.e. with the theory of a plurality of separate, though interdependent, elements (*dharma*). The phenomenon of knowledge was a compound phenomenon, resolvable into a number of elements simultaneously flashing into existence. Being conceived as momentary flashes, the elements could not move towards one another, could not come into contact, could not influence one another, there could be no " seizing " or " grasping " of the object by the intellect. But, according to the laws of interconnexion (*pratītya-samutpāda*) prevailing between them, some elements are invariably appearing accompanied by others arising in close contiguity with them. A moment of colour (*rūpa*), a moment of the sense-of-vision-matter (*cakṣuḥ*), and a moment of pure consciousness (*citta*), arising simultaneously in close contiguity, constitute what is called a sensation (*sparça*) [1] of colour. The element of consciousness according to the same laws never appears alone, but always supported by an object (*viṣaya*) and a receptive faculty (*indriya*).[2]

A very important, though somewhat scholastic, question is then raised : how is it that, if these three separate elements—the element colour, the element visual sense, and the element consciousness—merely appear, or flash, together, without being appurtenances of some non-existing living being, without being able to influence one another, to " grasp ", apprehend, or come into contact with one another—how is it, then, that there, nevertheless, is an " apprehending " of the object by the intellect ? Why is it that the resulting knowledge is a cognition " of colour ", and not a cognition of the visual sense,

[1] *Trayāṇāṃ sannipātaḥ sparçaḥ.* It is misleading to translate *sparça* by " contact ", since it represents a *caitta-dharma.*

[2] *Cakṣuḥ pratītya rūpaṃ ca cakṣur-vijñānam utpadyate.* Here *cakṣur-vijñāna* is not a visual sensation—that would be *sparça*—but a *pure sensation*, arising accompanied by a moment of the visual-sense-matter.

which is supposed to enter the combination on terms of equality with the other elements? The question about the relation between external (objective) and internal (subjective) element, and the "grasping" of the one by the other which was to have been evaded by the construction of a plurality of interdependent, but separate and equal, elements, reverts in another form. The answer is that, although there is no real coming in contact between elements, no grasping of the objective element by the intellect, nevertheless the three elements do not appear on terms of absolute equality; there is between two of them—consciousness and object—a special relation which might be termed "co-ordination" (*sārūpya*),[1] a relation which makes it possible that the complex phenomenon—the resulting cognition—is a cognition of colour and not of the visual sense.

Such an answer amounts, of course, to a confession of ignorance: this relation exists because it exists, it is required by the system, without this patchwork the system collapses. In all Indian—and, indeed, not only Indian—systems we always reach a point which must be acquiesced in without any possible justification. It must be assumed, not because it could be proved (*na sādhayituṃ çakyam*), but because there is no possibility of escape (*avarjanīyatayā*), it is a postulate of the system (*siddhānta-prasiddham*).

[1] This same *sārūpya* reappears in the transcendental system of Dignāga and Dharmakīrti, as it would seem, in a different, but similar, role of a salvage in extremis. Dharmakīrti establishes an absolute reality, the thing in itself, the single moment of pure sensation (*çuddhaṃ pratyakṣam = kalpanāpoḍham = svalakṣaṇam = kṣaṇa = paramārthasat*); this single moment of reality is the transcendental (*jñānena prāpayituṃ na çakyate*) reality underlying every representation with its complex of qualities, constructed by imagination (*kalpanā*). There is a difficulty in supplying some explanation of how this quite indefinite moment of pure sensation combines with the definite construction of reason, and *sārūpya* steps in to save the situation. Its role is consequently similar to Kant's schematism, that was intended to supply a bridge between pure sensation (reine Sinnlichkeit) and reason. Cf. my *Logic according to later Buddhists*, chap. on *pratykṣa*. About *sārūpya* in Sānkhya-Yoga see below, p. 64.

In the *Abhidharma-koça* we have the following account of the process of cognition [1] :—

Question.—We read in scripture, " Consciousness apprehends." What is consciousness here meant to do ?

Answer.—Nothing at all ! (It simply appears in co-ordination with its objective elements, like a result which is homogeneous with its cause.) When a result appears in conformity with its own cause it is doing nothing at all ; but we say that it does conform with it. Consciousness, likewise, appears in co-ordination (*sārūpya*) with its objective elements. It is (properly speaking) doing nothing. Nevertheless, we say that consciousness *does* cognize its object.

Question.—What is meant by " co-ordination " (between consciousness and its objective element) ?

Answer.—A conformity between them, the fact owing to which cognition, although caused (also) by the activity of the senses, is not something homogeneous with them. It is said to cognize the object and not the senses. (It bears the reflection of the objective element which is its corollary.) And, again, the expression " consciousness apprehends " is not inadequate, inasmuch as here also a continuity of conscious moments is the cause of every cognition. (" Consciousness apprehends " means that the previous moment is the cause of the following one.) The agent here also denotes simply the cause, just as in the current expression " the bell resounds " (the bell is doing nothing, but connected with it every following moment of sound is produced by the previous one). (We can give) another (illustration) : consciousness apprehends similarly to the way in which a light moves.

Question.—And how does a light move ?

Answer.—The light of a lamp is a common metaphorical designation for an uninterrupted production of a series of flashing flames. When this production changes its place, we say that the light has moved, (but in reality other flames have appeared in another place). Similarly, consciousness is a conventional name for a chain of conscious moments. When it changes its place (i.e. appears in co-ordination with another objective element) we say that it apprehends that object. And in the same way we are speaking about the existence of material elements. We

[1] *Ab. K.*, ix ; cf. *Soul Theory*, pp. 937-8.

say matter "is produced", it exists, but there is no difference between existence of an element and the element itself that *does* exist. The same applies to consciousness, (there is nothing that *does* cognize, apart from the evanescent flashings of consciousness itself).

The question of the reality of an outer world is, strictly speaking, obviated. In a system which denies the existence of a personality, splits everything into a plurality of separate elements, and admits of no real interaction between them, there is no possibility of distinguishing between an external and internal world. The latter does not exist, all elements are quite equally external towards one another. Nevertheless, the habit of distinguishing between internal and external, subjective and objective, could not be dropped altogether, and we meet with curious situations into which the philosopher is driven by logical deductions ; consciousness itself sometimes happens to be considered as an external element with regard to other elements. Such elements as ideas (*sanjñā*), feelings (*vedanā*), volitions (*cetanā*), and all forces (*saṃskāra*) are, as a rule, considered to be external elements. The *Abhidharma-koça* gives the following account of the question :—[1]

Question.—How many among the eighteen categories of elementary components (*dhātu*) of life are internal, how many external ?

Answer.—Internal are twelve, (the remaining six) colour, etc., are external.

Question.—Which are the twelve internal ones ?

Answer.—They are the six varieties of consciousness (*ṣaḍ-vijñāna-kāyāḥ*), i.e. consciousness (1) visual, (2) auditory, (3) olfactory, (4) gustatory, (5) tactile, (6) purely mental, and their six respective bases (*āçraya*) : the sense-organs of vision, audition, smelling, tasting, touch, and consciousness itself, i.e. its preceding moment (being the basic element of the next moment) —are internal. The remaining six, comprising visibility-matter (sounds, smells, tastes, tangibles, and mental or abstract objects, e.g. ideas), are external.

[1] *Ab. K.*, i, 39.

Question.—How is it possible for the elements of existence to be internal or external, if the Self (or the personality) in regard to which they should be external or internal does not exist at all ?

Answer.—Consciousness is metaphorically called a Self, because it yields some support to the (erroneous) idea of a Self. Buddha himself uses such expressions. He sometimes mentions control of the Self, (sometimes control of consciousness), e.g. " the wise man who has submitted *his Self* to strict control, migrates into heaven," and (in another place) He says : " the control of one's *consciousness* is a weal, the control of *consciousness* leads to bliss." The sense of vision and other sense-organs are the basic elements for the corresponding sensations ; consciousness, on the other hand, is the basic element for the perception of a Self. Therefore, as a consequence of this close connexion with consciousness, the sense-organs are brought under the head of internal elements.

A very characteristic question is then raised, namely, that this definition of an internal element does not apply to consciousness itself. If to be internal means merely to be the basic element of consciousness, as the organ of vision e.g. is the basic element (*āçraya*) for any visual consciousness, then, since consciousness could not be its own basis, it could neither be an internal element. The question is solved by stating that the preceding moment of consciousness is the basis for the following one and since time is irrelevant in this definition, consciousness must also be called internal. In any case, the *dharmāḥ* or *dharma-dhātu*, i.e. ideas and all mental phenomena and forces, are supposed to be external elements,[1] that is a postulate of the system.

The theory sketched above does not by any means prevent our using the expressions of common life with regard to an

[1] The exact division of the eighteen *dhātus* from this view-point is in—(1) Six bases, *āçraya-ṣaṭka, cakṣurādi* : organs of sense and consciousness (*manaḥ*), otherwise called *ṣaḍ indriyāṇi*, or the six faculties. (2) Six " based ", *āçrita-ṣaṭka, cakṣur-vijñānādi* : five varieties of sensation and intellectual consciousness (*mano-vijñāna*). (3) Six cognized objects (*ālambana-ṣaṭka* and *viṣaya-ṣaṭka*) : five varieties of sense objects and mental objects ; they are, with regard to the second set, *ālambanas*, and *viṣayas* with regard to the *indriyas*.

inter-action or contact between sense-organ and object. We meet even with the comparison of this contact to a clash of butting goats, but these expressions need not be taken literally. About the possibility of any real contact between the sense-organ and its object, we find the following explanations.[1] The senses are divided into two sets according to their power of acting at a distance, or through contact only. The senses of vision and audition apprehend their objects at a distance. For the eye a distance is even a necessary condition, because e.g. a drop of medicine introduced into the eye cannot be seen by it. The three organs of smelling, tasting, and touch must be in immediate contact with the object. The question is then raised, how is contact possible if there is no movement, and it is answered that contact is only a name for production of two elements in immediate vicinity. The question of contact between object and organ of sense affords an opportunity for debating the question of contact between objects in general. The Vaibhāṣikas maintain that when there is a contact, i.e. simultaneous production of two things in close vicinity, their vicinity is absolute, there is nothing between, but Vasubandhu objects that absolute vicinity is impossible for many reasons. He quotes the opinion of two celebrated philosophers, Vasumitra and Bhadanta; the first says: "If the atoms of which the objects are composed could really come into contact, they would be existing during the next moment," i.e. since every atom is but a momentary flashing, its coming into contact is impossible; the contact will be achieved by another atom appearing in the next moment. Bhadanta says: "There is no such thing as contact. Contact is only a name for the close vicinity (of two apparitions)." [2]

With regard to matter (*rūpa*), the *Abhidharma-koça* gives two different standpoints from which to consider its position as either external or internal. It is external if part of another's personality (*saṃtāna*), his faculties or his objects, internal if

[1] *Ab. K.*, ad i, 43, Tibetan text, p. 82, 5 ff.

[2] *Nirantara-utpāda*, ibid., Tibetan text, p. 83, 9.

part of my own personality, my faculties or my objects. Otherwise it may be distinguished according to the classification into "bases" (*āyatana*) of cognition. As we have seen, this classification divides everything according to the faculties by which it is perceived: the five sense-organs (*indriya*) are internal bases (*adhyātmāyatana*) and the objective sense-data represent the external ones (*bāhyāyatana*).[1]

Since there is no real difference of external and internal, the senses do not really play any part in perception; they are mere facts or elements that appear together with other elements according to laws of interconnexion. If we speak of the sense of vision as perceiving colour, this must not be taken literally. There is in the *Abhidharma-koça*[2] a long discussion about the relative parts of the two elements, of the visual sense and of consciousness, in the process of perception. First an idealist opponent maintains that consciousness alone produces cognition, the part of the senses is *nil*. This opinion is disposed of by pointing to the fact that consciousness does not apprehend objects behind a wall, which it ought to have achieved if it were independent of the sense-organs.[3] The Sarvāstivādin then reviews several explanations of the difference between the parts of the sense-organ and consciousness in perception. "We find in Scripture," he says, the following statement":—

"This, O Brahmin, is the organ of vision; it is a door through which to see colours and shapes." This means that consciousness perceives (colours) through the organ of vision (which is comparable to a door). It, strictly speaking, means that when we use

[1] Cf. *Ab. K.*, i, 20. For the position in the Pali canon cf. Mrs. C. Rhys Davids, *Buddhist Psychology*, p. 140 ff. The idea that external matter is the matter entering into the scope of another person's life may be traced in the *Vibhanga*, where exterior *rūpa* is said to be the interior *rūpa* of another person: *rūpaṃ bahidhā yaṃ rūpaṃ teṣaṃ teṣaṃ parasattānaṃ* (? *parasaṃtānānaṃ*) *parapuggalānaṃ*, etc. Cf. likewise Majjhima, i, 421 ff. (No. 2 Mahārāhulovādasutta).

[2] *Ab. K.*, i, 42, Tibetan text, p. 77, 10 ff.

[3] Ibid., Tibetan text, p. 78, 11 ff.

the verb " to see " we only indicate that there is an (open) door (for the consciousness to apprehend a colour). It is wrong to maintain that the organ of vision (*cakṣuḥ*) " looks " (*paçyati*), with the result that it " sees ", (perception is produced only by the element of consciousness).

Question.—If it is the element of consciousness that " sees ", who is it that becomes conscious (of the thing seen) ? What is the difference between these two expressions, " to see a colour " and " to become conscious of the presence of a colour " ?

Answer.—Although that (element) which produces consciousness cannot, strictly speaking, be supposed " to see ", nevertheless both expressions are used indiscriminately: " he sees " and " he is conscious of ", just as with regard to understanding (*prajñā*) we may equally use the expressions " he sees it " and " he understands it ".

The Sarvāstivādin then states that the elements of visual sense and consciousness do not exhibit any agency, they simply appear under certain conditions: the organ of sense and the object being present, consciousness arises, and the mere fact of its apparition is tantamount to a sensation of colour, just as the sun in arising produces the day; it does nothing, but its appearance itself is the day. The Sautrāntika adheres to the same opinion, and winds up with the remark: " What is the use of this quarrel about 'who sees' and 'who is conscious'? It is like chewing empty space! A visual perception (sensation) is a fact, conditioned by two other facts, an organ of vision and some colour. Which is the agent? What is the agency? Useless questions! There is nothing but the elementary facts (*dharma-mātram*) appearing as cause and effect. In practice, according to the requirements of the case, we may use either the expression 'the eye sees' or 'consciousness is being aware'. But we should not attach great importance to these expressions. Buddha himself has declared, 'do not stick to the expressions used by common people, do not attach any importance to usual terms!' 'The eye sees,' 'the ear hears,' 'the nose smells,' 'the tongue tastes,' 'the body feels,' 'the intellect becomes conscious,' the Kaçmirian Vaibhāṣikas make use of these expressions (without taking them literally)." [1]

This sounds like an answer to the Sānkhya philosophers. They maintained that the sense organ "sees", but consciousness "is conscious".[2] The Mimāṃsakas adopted the same view in admitting an indistinct sense-perception (*ālocana*) comparable to the perceptions of a child and the clear vision with participation by the understanding.[3] The transcendental school of Dharmakīrti denied the difference. It maintained that, distinct or indistinct, the fact of knowledge remained the same in its essence.[4]

There is no great disagreement between the Vaibhāṣikas (Sarvāstivādins) and the Sautrāntikas on the interpretation of the origin of cognition. It is in their opinion a complex phenomenon in which several elements participate, interconnected, but separate, with the essential presence of the element of consciousness among them.[5]

In the light of this theory of cognition it is surprising to see the family-likeness which reveals itself between the consciousness (*cit, puruṣa*) of the Sānkhyas and its Buddhist counterpart (*vijñāna*). Both are absolutely inactive, without any content, a knowledge without an object, a knowledge "of nothing", pure sensation, mere awareness, a substance without either qualities or movements. Being the pure light of knowledge it "stands by" the phenomena, illuminates them, reflects them, without grasping them or being affected by them.[6] The only difference is that in Sānkhya it represents an eternal principle, whereas in Buddhism momentary light-flashes appearing at the time when certain other

[1] *Ab. K.*, i, 42, Tibetan text, p. 79, 18.

[2] Garbe, *Sānkhya Philosophie*, 2nd ed., pp. 319 ff., 326.

[3] *Çlokavārtika, Pratyakṣasūtra.*

[4] *Nyāyabindut.*, p. 4 ff.

[5] The information about the Sautrāntika theory of cognition, contained in the *Sarva-darçana-sangraha* and similar works (*bāhyārthānumeyatva*), reposes on a confusion by Brahmanical authors between Sautrāntika and Vijñāna-vāda, not seldom to be met with.

[6] Garbe, op. cit., pp. 358 ff.

elements are present.[1] The order which it occupies among the Buddhist groups (*skandhas*) of elements is likewise suggestive. It is not included in the mental groups. It has a place of its own just at the end of the list, similar to the position occupied by it as the twenty-fifth principle of Sānkhya.[2] In order to avoid the difficulty involved in the idea of one element "grasping" the other, it is imagined that there is the mere fact of them being near one another.[3] Whatsoever that may mean in Yoga, in Buddhism it refers to interconnected flashings into existence of two elements. Their relation of subject and object, nevertheless, remains unexplained, and this fact is christened by the name of "co-ordination" (*sārūpya*). We meet the same *deus ex mahina* performing an analogous task in both systems; subject and object stand aloof from one another, yet they are "co-ordinated".[4]

It can hardly be doubted that the emphatic denial of any difference between consciousness, mind, and intellect [5] in Buddhism is likewise a direct reply to the Sānkhya system, where we find such a gap between consciousness and mind, and the latter then divided into the threefold internal organ.

The doctrine of identity between consciousness and an internal organ of knowledge is characteristic for Buddhism from its very beginning. It is, in fact, another manner of expressing the denial of a soul and is the direct consequence of its being replaced by separate elements. We find it clearly stated in the oldest texts.[6] It probably was, at the time, a new doctrine, intended to replace an older one. The

[1] *Sānkhya-karikā*, 64, which has given an opportunity to impute to the system the negation of a soul, only proves that the conscious principle deprived of any characteristic or content, represents in Sānkhya nothing else than pure sensation, or pure consciousness. Cf. Garbe, op. cit., p. 364.

[2] About the order in which the *skandhas* stand we find a great many speculations in *Ab. K.*, i, 22; cf. Mrs. C. Rhys Davids, *B. Psych.*, p. 54.

[3] Vyāsa, ad i, 4; ii, 23.

[4] Professor J. H. Woods translates "correlation", which is much the same (op. cit., p. 14, 160 ff.).

[5] *Ab. K.*, ii, 34; Mrs. C. Rhys Davids, *B. Psych.*, p. 66.

[6] *Saṃyutta*, ii, 94; *Majjhim.*, i, 256 ff.

pre-Buddhistic use of the terms is clearly discernible in the Pali texts. One or the other of these synonymous terms is used with preference in certain contexts.[1] As an organ (*indriya, āyatana* No. 6) and as a common resort (*pratisaraṇa*) for the sense-organs, the term "mind" (*manaḥ*) is preferred; consciousness purely mental, non-sensuous, is called *mano-vijñāna* (*dhātu* No. 18), i.e. consciousness arising, not from an organ of sense, but from consciousness itself, from its preceding moment, when the preceding moment takes the place of a support (*āçraya*), or an organ (*indriya*), for a non-sensuous idea. These distinctions are mere traces of older habits of thought. The philosophical atmosphere in the time of Buddha was in all probability saturated with Sānkhya ideas. Buddhism cannot be fully understood if these connexions are not taken into account.

XV. Pre-Buddhaic Buddhism

Can the theory sketched above be characterized as a system of realism? It is certainly not the naive realism of Nyāya-Vaiçeṣika. For the Brahmanical writers it was realism (*bāhyārthāstitva*) because it was different from the later, more definite, idealism. But the difference between *Sarvāstivāda* and *Vijñānavāda* consists rather in that the former is pluralistic and the latter converts all elements into aspects of one store-consciousness (*ālaya-vijñāna*). The whole system of elements is retained with slight variations. Professor O. Rosenberg is inclined to conclude that in theory of cognition the Buddhists were idealists from the beginning, but they were realists so far as they accepted the real existence of a transcendental absolute reality.[2] It has, in any case, a position of its own, very far from ordinary realism, resembling perhaps some modern theories which accept the reality of external as well as internal facts and a certain "co-ordination" between

[1] Mrs. C. Rhys Davids, op. cit., pp. 17 ff., has with very fine discrimination traced the different shades of meaning conveyed in the Pali canonical texts by these terms, which are emphatically declared to be synonymous.

[2] Op. cit., chap. viii.

them, without the one "grasping" the other. The cinematographic representation of the world and the converting of all the facts of the inner and outer world composing an individual stream of life into a complex play of interconnected momentary flashes, is anything but realism. The world is a mirage. The reality underlying it is beyond our cognition. Nāgārjuna gave the right explanation in calling it an empty (*çūnya*) illusion (*māyā*). Professor O. Rosenberg insists upon the illusionistic tendency of Buddhism from the very outset.[1] Even for Buddhaghoṣa not only outer objects, but men were nothing but puppets trying to deceive us as to their reality.[2] That Çankara established his illusionistic doctrine of Vedānta under Buddhist influence is at present more or less generally accepted. But we must make the difference between the radical illusionism of Çankara and Nāgarjuna and the half-way illusionism of primitive Buddhism. The visible world was, as Vācaspatimiçra [3] says with reference to Sānkhya-Yoga, similar to an illusion, but not exactly an illusion (*māyeva na tu māyā*). The position of the Sānkhya, accepting the transcendental elements (*guṇas*) as the only reality, was just the same.

Whether the *anātma-dharma* theory was the personal creation of Çākyamuni Buddha himself, or not, is a quite irrelevant question. In any case, we do not know of any form

[1] Op. cit., chaps. iv, viii, and xviii.

[2] *Visuddhi-magga*, xi, Warren, *Buddhism*, p. 158. Mrs. C. Rhys Davids, op. cit., denies in primitive Buddhism both illusionism (p. 65) and idealism (p. 75). When the root of phenomenal existence is declared to be illusion (*avidyā*), and the process of life is "empty with a twelvefold emptiness" (*Visuddhi-M.*, xvii, Warren, op. cit., p. 175), it is difficult to deny illusionism altogether. As to the different interpretations of illusion cf. S. Dasgupta, *History*, p. 384. Professor O. Rosenberg's chief argument in favour of idealism was drawn from the fact that the objects of the outer world were components of one *saṃtāna*, i.e. internal to the personality. But, considering that in primitive Buddhism all elements are equally external to one another and *saṃtāna* is not a reality, not a *dharma*, there is no idealism in the later sense. The interpretation admitted by Mrs. Rhys Davids, p. 75, namely, that "the microcosm (i.e. *pudgala*) apprehended the macrocosm by way of its sense-doors", looks dangerously like *satkāyadṛṣti*!

[3] *Vyāsa*, iv, 13.

of Buddhism without this doctrine and its corollary classifications of elements into *skandha*, *āyatana*, and *dhātu*, the laws of their interconnexion (*pratītya-samutpāda*), and the complicated constructions which these termini involve. This is also, as Professor O. Rosenberg rightly remarks, the common foundation of all the forms of Buddhism in all the countries where this religion flourishes at present. Failing to realize that, some superficial observers concluded that in the northern countries Buddhism was "degenerate" and altogether a different religion. It is a salient feature of Indian philosophy that its history splits into several independent lines of development which run parallel from an early beginning down to modern times. Each development has its own fundamental idea to start with, and the development makes every effort to keep faithful to the start. Thus we have the realism (*ārambha-vāda*) of the Vaiçeṣika, the pluralism (*sanghāta-vāda*) of Buddhism, the evolutionism (*pariṇāma-vāda*) of Sānkhya-Yoga, and the illusionism (*vivarta-vāda*) of Vedānta running in parallel lines of development from the remotest antiquity, each with its own ontology, its own theory of causation, its own theory of cognition, its own idea of salvation, and its own idea of the origin of the limitations (*avidyā*) of our experience.

We know of celebrated philosophers who have been engaged in more than one line, but the lines were always kept separate. In Buddhism the development began in the discussions of the early Hīnayāna schools. The Sarvāstivādins established a catalogue of seventy-five elements. The Sautrāntikas excluded a number of them as mere names; the Mādhyamikas viewed all of them as contingent (*çūnya*) upon one another, and therefore declared the world to be an illusion; the Vijñānavādins converted them into ideas, aspects of one store-consciousness (*ālaya-vijñāna*), but the pluralistic fundamental idea remained; its idealistic and illusionistic tendency, which was clear from the beginning, was elaborately worked out by later scholars.

The possibility is not precluded that the foundation stone of the *anātma-dharma* theory was laid before Buddha. Just as Mahāvīra was not the first to proclaim Jainism, but only adopted and gave lustre to a doctrine which existed before him, just so Buddha may have adopted and spread a doctrine which he found somewhere in that philosophical laboratory which was the India of his time. He, indeed, is reported to have emphatically disowned the authorship of a new teaching, but claimed to be the follower of a doctrine established long ago by former Buddhas. This is usually interpreted as a kind of propaganda device, but it is not quite improbable that a real historical fact underlies these assertions.

Among that oldest set of Upaniṣads which for many reasons are generally admitted to be pre-Buddhistic, but display some knowledge of the Sānkhya system, we find, along with Sānkhya conceptions, a statement that might be an indication of the existence of such a pre-Buddhistic form of the *anātma-dharma* theory. In the *Kāṭhakopaniṣad*, which belongs to this class, a doctrine is mentioned that is evidently strongly opposed to the monistic view of an immortal soul (*ātman*), and favours instead a theory of separate elements (*pṛthag-dharmān paçyati*). This theory is repudiated with the following remark: "Just as rainwater that has fallen down in a desert is scattered and lost among the undulations of the ground, just so is (a philosopher) who maintains the existence of separate elements lost in running after nothing else but these (separate elements)."[1]

Professor H. Jacobi has shown that unorthodox opinions, opposed to the accepted soul-theory, are alluded to even in the oldest set of the Upaniṣads.[2] These indications are made in the usual Upaniṣad style and anything but precise.

What emerges from the passage of the *Kāṭhaka* cited above is that there was a doctrine opposed to the reigning soul-

[1] *Kāṭhakop.*, iv, 14; cf. Mrs. and Professor W. Geiger, op. cit., p. 9. In another passage of the same text (i, 21) *dharma* apparently also means an element, but a subtle and immortal one.

[2] Ernst Kuhn memorial volume (Munich, 1916), p. 38.

theory, that it maintained the existence of subtle elements and separate elements (*pṛthag dharma*), and that such a doctrine, in the opinion of the author, did not lead to salvation. Çankara, in his commentary, agrees that Buddhism is alluded to, but, very bluntly, he interprets *dharma* as meaning here individual soul.[1] As a matter of fact, *dharma* never occurs with this meaning in the Upaniṣads. Its occurrence in the *Kāṭhaka* leaves the impression that it is a catchword, referring to a foreign and new doctrine, some *anātma-dharma* theory.[2]

Professor Jacobi,[3] in a recent work, arrives at the conclusion that at the epoch of which the *Kāṭhaka* is the most characteristic exponent the theory of an immortal individual soul was a new idea which, in all probability, enjoyed great popularity as a novelty and met with general approval.

[1] In his commentary on the *Gauḍapāda Kārikā*, where the term *dharma* occurs, very clearly in the sense the *Mādhyamika* interpretation has given it, namely, as something unreal, a mere illusion, the real or the pseudo-Çankara likewise enforces the meaning of an individual soul.

[2] There are no traces of the Buddhist meaning of *dharma* having been known to Pāṇini, but there are some traces with regard to its corollary, the term *saṃskāra* or *saṃskṛta*. When causation is to be expressed, he makes a difference between real efficiency, i.e. one fact transgressing its own existence and affecting the other, which he calls *pratiyatna*, explained as *guṇāntarādhāna* (the same as *atiçayādhāna*, *parasparopakāra*, or simply *upakāra*), and an efficiency which is contrasted with it and conceived as two separate facts conditioning one another which he simply calls *saṃskṛta*; it is explained as *sata utkarṣādhānaṃ saṃskāraḥ*, i.e. "a force is what produces (= conditions) an enhancement in (some) existent." In the first case, *upakṛta* or *upaskṛta* is used, in the second *saṃskṛta*, cf. ii, 3, 53; vi, 1, 139; iv, 2, 16; iv, 4, 3; cf. the *Kāçikā*. That the two *paribhāṣās*, *guṇāntarādhānam* and *sata utkarṣādhānaṃ saṃskāraḥ*, refer to the Sānkhya and Buddhist views respectively is probable. In later literature the difference between *upakāra* and simple *saṃskāra* is frequently referred to, cf. *Nyāyab'nduṭīkā*, ed. Peterson (*Bibl. Ind.*), p. 13: *dvividhaç ca sahakārī parasparopakārī* . . .; cf. *Six Buddhist Nyāya Tracts*, p. 48 ff., *Sarvadarçana-sangraha*, p. 10 (*Bibl. Ind.*): *sahakāriṇaḥ kim bhāvasya upakurvanti na vā*. That the philosophical conceptions involved in this difference were known to Pāṇini would appear from the suggestive word *pratiyatna* = *upakāra*, as opposed to *saṃskāra*, but this is by no means certain. The conception of *guṇāntara-yoga* = *vikāra* is mentioned in *M. bhāṣya*, ad v, 1, 2. A similar contrast lies in *adhītya-* versus *pratītya-samutpāda*, cf. *Bh. jāla-sutta*.

[3] *Die indische Philosophie* in *Das Licht des Ostens* (Stuttgart, 1922).

There is, indeed, a wide gap between this class of Upaniṣads and the older set, a difference in style, terminology, and the whole intellectual atmosphere. The idea of a surviving personality, of a Self and even a Universal Self, is not unknown in the Veda: its essence and its relation to Brahma is the main topic of discussion in the Upaniṣads. But this Self is a psycho-physical entity, different explanations of its nature are proposed, and materialistic views are not excluded. The idea of an immortal soul in our sense, a spiritual monad, a simple, uncomposite, eternal, immaterial substance is quite unknown in the Veda, inclusive of the older Upaniṣads. The new conception was accepted by the Jains, the Sānkhyas, Mīmāṃsakas, and later by all philosophical systems except the materialists and the Buddhists. In the Sānkhya the old theory survived, in the shape of the *linga-çarīra*, along with the adoption of the new. The attitude of Buddhism towards both the old and the new theories was that of a most emphatic denial. Scholars were always struck by the spirit of extreme animosity which undoubtedly reveals itself in the oldest Buddhist texts whenever the idea of a soul is mentioned. In the light of Professor Jacobi's hypothesis this may find a natural explanation in the feeling of excitement with which the new theory was met and assailed by its chief opponents, for which mere theoretical considerations of abstract argument seem insufficient to account. In Buddhist records we find the old and the new soul-theories clearly distinguished. The doctrine which maintains the reality of a Self corresponding to the psycho-physical individual is called *ātma-vāda*, whereas the view approaching the doctrine of a permanent Soul is *pudgala-vāda*. All Buddhists rejected the *ātma-vāda*, since Buddhism (*buddhānuçāsanī*), philosophically, means nothing else than the *dharmatā*, the theory of *dharmas*, which is but another name for *anātman, nairātmya*. But there are two schools—the Vātsīputrīyas and the Sammitīyas—which are, nevertheless, adherents of the *pudgala-vāda*. According to the exposition of Vasubandhu, this means that the *internal skandhas* at a given moment constitute a certain unity, which is related to them as fire to fuel.[1] It had not the absolute reality of a *dharma*, it was not included in the lists of *dharmas*, but, nevertheless, it was not quite unreal. This *pudgala* was also regarded as surviving, since it is maintained that it assumes new elements at birth and throws them off at death.[2] The *pudgala* of a Buddha seems to be an Omniscient Eternal Spirit.[3] The sūtra of the burden-bearer, where *pudgala* is compared with the bearer and the *skandhas* with the burden, was invoked as a proof that Buddha himself admitted some reality of the *pudgala*.[4] For all the other Buddhist schools *pudgala* was but another name for *ātman*, and they refuted both theories by the same arguments. That the position of the Vātsīputrīyas was wrong, i.e. not in strict conformity with the *dharma*-theory, is evident, since this theory admits no real unity whatsoever between separate elements. Therefore Self, Soul, personality, individual, living being, human being—all these conceptions do not answer to ultimate realities: they are but names for some combinations of *dharmas*, i.e. formulas of elements.[5] If our supposition that the *anātma-dharma* theory is mentioned in the *Kāṭhakopaniṣad* is correct, it evidently was directed against both the old and the new Soul-theories as equally unacceptable. But, on the other hand, the tenacious effort of some Buddhist schools to save the idea of some real unity between the elements of a personal life,[6] or the idea of a spiritual principle governing it, is partly due to the difficulty of the problem and partly to an old tradition. We find, indeed, in the Brāhmaṇas and the

[1] *Soul Theory*, p. 830.

[2] Ibid., p. 851.

[3] Ibid., p. 841.

[4] Ibid., p. 842. Udyotakara, in his exposition of *ātma-vāda* (pp. 338–49), likewise mentions this sūtra as contradicting the doctrine of *anātman*.

[5] Ibid., p. 838.

[6] The Sarvāstivādins explained the union of the elements in a personality by the operation of a special force (*saṃskāra*), which they named *prāpti*; cf. above, p. 23, and in the tables of elements in the Appendix II, where it is found under *viprayukta-saṃskāra*, No. 1.

Upaniṣads something like a forerunner of the Buddhist *skandhas*. The individual is also composed of elements; during his lifetime they are united; the union ceases at death, and through a reunion of them a new life begins.[1] Curiously enough, the number of these elements, or factors, as Professor Jacobi prefers to translate the term *prāṇa*, is the same as the number of the Buddhist *skandhas*. The elements themselves are quite different, and this difference bears witness of the enormous progress achieved by Indian philosophy during the time between the primitive Upaniṣads and the rise of Buddhism. In the Buddhist system we have a division of mental faculties into feeling, concept, will, and pure sensation, in which modern psychology would not have much to change. In the Upaniṣads it is a very primitive attempt, giving breath, speech, sense of vision, sense of audition and intellect as the elements. But one point of similarity remains: the last and, evidently, the most important element is in both cases *manas*. The makrocosm, or the Universal Soul, is likewise analysed by the Upaniṣads into five component elements.[2] In the number of the Buddhist *skandhas* and in the position of *manas* (= *vijñāna*) among them we probably have the survival of an old tradition.[3] It is only by such an indirect influence that we can explain the astonishing fact of the simultaneous existence of different classifications of the elements for which there is no intrinsic requirement in the system. When the *anātma-dharma* theory was definitely framed, with its theory of causation and theory of cognition, the classification of elements into "bases" of cognition (*āyatana*) became quite natural and indispensable,

[1] H. Jacobi, op. cit., p. 146. Cf. H. Oldenberg, *Die Weltanschauung der Brāhmaṇa-Texte*, pp. 88 ff., 234.

[2] H. Jacobi, op. cit., p. 146. Cf. H. Oldenberg, *Die Lehre der Upanishaden*, p. 54.

[3] A similar relation, as is generally admitted, exists between the three elements *tejas*, *āpas*, *annam* of the *Chāndogya*, vi, and the three *guṇas* of the Sānkhyas.

but the classification into *skandhas* was useless. It, nevertheless, was retained in compliance with an old habit of thought, and such changes as were required by the progress of philosophic analysis were introduced.

Thus it is that the fundamental idea of Buddhism—a plurality of separate elements without real unity—had its roots in the primitive speculations of the Upaniṣads. At the time when a new conception of the Soul was elaborated in Brahmanical circles, some kind of pre-Buddhaic Buddhism, under which we understand the *anātma-dharma* theory, must have been already in existence. This time is the epoch of the *Kāṭhakopaniṣad*, which, as Professor Jacobi points out,[1] might also be the time of pre-Jinistic Jainism, the time of Pārçvanātha, i.e. the eighth century B.C.

XVI. Summary

To summarize :-

The conception of a *dharma* is the central point of the Buddhist doctrine. In the light of this conception Buddhism discloses itself as a metaphysical theory developed out of one fundamental principle, viz. the idea that existence is an interplay of a plurality of subtle, ultimate, not further analysable elements of Matter, Mind, and Forces. These elements are technically called *dharmas*, a meaning which this word has in this system alone. Buddhism, accordingly, can be characterized as a system of Radical Pluralism (*sanghāta-vāda*)[2]: the elements alone are realities, every combination of them is a mere name covering a plurality of separate elements. The moral teaching of a path towards Final Deliverance is not something additional or extraneous to this ontological doctrine, it is most intimately connected with it and, in fact, identical with it.

[1] Op. cit., p. 150.

[2] As contrasted with the *ārambha-vāda*, which maintains the reality of the whole as well as of the elements, and the *pariṇāma-vāda*, which ascribes absolute reality only to the whole.

The connotation of the term *dharma* implies that—

1. Every element is a separate (*pṛthak*) entity or force.

2. There is no inherence of one element in another, hence no substance apart from its qualities, no Matter beyond the separate sense-data, and no Soul beyond the separate mental data (*dharma* = *anātman* = *nirjīva*).

3. Elements have no duration, every moment represents a separate element; thought is evanescent, there are no moving bodies, but consecutive appearances, flashings, of new elements in new places (*kṣaṇikatva*).

4. The elements co-operate with one another (*saṃskṛta*).

5. This co-operating activity is controlled by the laws of causation (*pratītya-samutpāda*).

6. The world-process is thus a process of co-operation between seventy-two kinds of subtle, evanescent elements, and such is the nature of *dharmas* that they proceed from causes (*hetu-prabhava*) and steer towards extinction (*nirodha*).

7. Influenced (*sāsrava*) by the element *avidyā*, the process is in full swing. Influenced by the element *prajñā*, it has a tendency towards appeasement and final extinction. In the first case streams (*santāna*) of combining elements are produced which correspond to ordinary men (*pṛthag-jana*); in the second the stream represents a saint (*ārya*). The complete stoppage of the process of phenomenal life corresponds to a Buddha.

8. Hence the elements are broadly divided into unrest (*duḥkha*), cause of unrest (*duḥkha-samudaya* = *avidyā*), extinction (*nirodha*), and cause of extinction (*mārga* = *prajñā*).

9. The final result of the world-process is its suppression, Absolute Calm: all co-operation is extinct and replaced by immutability (*asaṃskṛta* = *nirvāṇa*).

Since all these particular doctrines are logically developed out of one fundamental principle, Buddhism can be resolved in a series of equations:—

dharmatā = *nairātmya* = *kṣaṇikatva* = *saṃskṛtatva* =

pratītya-samutpannatva = *sāsrava-anāsravatva* = *saṃkleça-vyavadānatva* = *duḥkha-nirodha* = *saṃsāra-nirvāṇa*.

But, although the conception of an element of existence has given rise to an imposing superstructure in the shape of a consistent system of philosophy, its inmost nature remains a riddle. What is *dharma* ? It is inconceivable ! It is subtle ! No one will ever be able to tell what its real nature (*dharma-svabhāva*) is ! It is transcendental !

APPENDIX I

Vasubandhu on the Fundamental Principle of the Sarvāstivāda School

The fifth chapter (*koça-sthāna*) of the *Abhidharma-koça* (v, 24–6) contains a detailed exposition of the argument between the Sarvāstivādins or Vaibhāṣikas and the Sautrāntikas upon the question of the reality of future and past elements (*dharmas*), written according to the method of later dialectics. It is divided in two parts, *pūrvapakṣa* and *uttarapakṣa*. In the first the Vaibhāṣika makes a statement of his case, and he is attacked by the Sautrāntika; he answers the questions and triumphs over the opponent. In the second the parts are reversed: the Vaibhāṣika puts the questions and the Sautrāntika answers them and secures the final victory. As a conclusion the Vaibhāṣika gives voice to his despair at the impossibility of conceiving the transcendentally deep essence of the elements of existence. The translation is made from the Tibetan text of the Peking edition of the Bstan-ḫgyur, Mdo, vol. 64, fol. 279, b. 5–285, a. 2. Some explanations have been introduced from Yaçomitra's Commentary, and the Tibetan commentary of Mchims-pa, which is the standard work for *abhidharma* throughout Mongolia and Tibet.

An Episodical Investigation into the Possibility of Past and Future Efficiency

(*Abhidharma-koça, Kārikās V*, 24–6)

(The author establishes that some passions exist only at the time when the corresponding objects are present, such are love or disgust towards sense-objects. But there are other passions of a general scope, such as preconceived dogmatical ideas, delusion, a doubting turn of mind, etc.; these have a bearing towards all objects whether past, present, or future. The following question is then raised,)

Bstan-ḫgyur, 64, f. 279, b. 5.

But are this past and this future really existent or not? If they are, it would follow that the elementary forces (*saṃskāra*) (which are active in the process of life) must be permanent (i.e. immovable), since they exist through all time. If they are not, how is it to be explained that a man is attracted to (objects past and future) by such (passion as he experienced formerly, or will be subject to in future)?

The *Vaibhāṣikas* do not admit those elements (which combine in the process of life) to be permanent, since they are subject (to the action of four energies which are) the characteristic appurtenance of such elements (viz. the forces of origination, decay, existence, and destruction). But, on the other hand, they emphatically declare that "the times" (i.e. everyone of the three times) are existent in reality.

The *Sautrāntika* asks, for what reason?

(PART I.—*The case for Everlasting Elements*)

The *Vaibhāṣika* answers: The times are always existent (1) because this has been declared in Scripture, (2) because of the double (cause of perception), (3) because of the existence of the perception's object, (4) because of the production of a result (by previous deeds). Since we maintain that all this exists, we profess the theory that everything exists (*Sarvāstivāda*). Kārikā, v, 24.

(1) *Because this has been declared in Scripture.*—Our Sublime Lord has declared: ("the elements of matter, O Brethren, the past and the future ones, are impermanent, not to speak of, the present ones. This is perceived by the perfect saint, endowed, as he is, with wisdom. Therefore, he is regardless of past sense-objects, he does not rejoice at future enjoyments, he entertains disgust and aversion in regard to the present ones, he is engaged in keeping them off). O Brethren! if some kind of past matter did not exist, the perfect saint endowed with wisdom could not be regardless of past sense-objects, but, since they are existent, he (enjoys the privilege of) disregarding them. If some kind of future matter were not existent, the wise and perfect saint could not be free from rejoicing at future enjoyments (since his independence would have no object). But future sense-objects do exist, etc." 279, b. 7. Yaçom. 279, b. 7

(2) *Because of the double (cause of perception).*—It is declared in Scripture: "consciousness, when operating, is conditioned by (elements) of a double kind." What are they? The sense of vision and colour (for a visual consciousness), and so on (an organ of perception and its respective object for each of the six kinds 280, a. 2.

of consciousness, the last being) the intellect itself and its non-sensuous objects[1] (for consciousness purely mental).

Thus these first two reasons for admitting the existence of the past and the future are taken from Scripture, but there are others, too, which are founded on argument.

280, a. 4. (3) *Because of the existence of an object.*—If there is an object, its cognition can arise; if there is none, neither can its cognition be produced. If the past and the future were not existent, the objects (of the corresponding cognition) would be non-existent, and, as non-existent, they could not be cognized.

(4) *Because of the production of a result* (*by former deeds*).—If the past did not exist, how could a deed, good or bad, attain, after some lapse of time, its fruition, since, at the time when the
Yaçom. latter appears, the cause which has produced retribution is gone. (A former deed, good or bad, does exist in reality, because, when it becomes ripe, it produces fruition, just as a present one does.)

280, a. 6. For these reasons we *Vaibhāṣikas* maintain that the past and the future necessarily exist. This leads to the theory that everything is existent, and our school is known by emphatically adhering to the principle of such universal existence (*Sarvāstivāda*). Accordingly (it is said above in the mnemonic verse): "since we maintain that all this exists, we profess the theory that everything exists." Those who maintain that everything, past, future, and present, exists are advocates of universal existence (*Sarvāstivādins*). On the other hand, those who make a distinction, partly admitting and partly denying this theory, are termed the Distinguishing School (*Vibhajyavādins*). They maintain that the present elements, and those among the past that have not yet produced their fruitions, are existent, but they deny the existence of the future ones and of those among the past that have already produced fruition.[2]

280, b. 2. *Sautrāntika.*—And how many branches are there among these advocates of universal existence?

Kārikā, v, 25. *Vaibhāṣika.*—There are four branches, inasmuch as they maintain (1) a change of existence (*bhāva-pariṇāma*), (2) a change of aspect (*lakṣaṇa-pariṇāma*), (3) a change of condition (*avasthā-pariṇāma*), or (4) contingency (*apekṣā-pariṇāma*). The third is

[1] *Manaḥ* and *dharmāḥ*.
[2] Cf. above, p. 43, n. 3.

all right. The difference in time reposes on a difference of condition (i.e. function of the elements).

(1) It was the venerable Dharmatrāta who maintained the view that existence (*bhāva*) changes in the course of time, not substance (*dravya*). He is known to have been arguing thus: when an element enters different times, its existence changes, but not its essence, just as when a golden vessel is broken, its form changes, but not its colour. And when milk is turned into curds, its taste, consistency, and digestive value are gone, but not its colour.[1] In the same manner, when an element, after having been future, enters into a present time, it gets rid of its future existence, but not of the existence of its essence, and when from present it becomes past, it casts away its present existence, but not the existence of its substance. 280, b. 3.

(2) It was the venerable Ghoṣa who assumed a change in the aspect of the elements (*lakṣaṇa*). He is known to have professed the theory that, when an element appears at different times, the past one retains its past aspect, without being severed from its future and present aspects, the future has its future aspect, without being altogether deprived of its past and present aspects, the present likewise retains its present aspect, without completely losing its past and future aspects. Just as, when a man falls into passionate love with a female, he is not altogether deprived of his capacity of love towards other females (but this capacity is not prominent). 280, b. 6.

(3) A change of condition (*avasthā*) is advocated by the venerable Vasumitra. He is known to have maintained that, when one element manifests itself at different times, it changes in condition, and receives different designations according to the condition which it has reached, without changing in substance. 281, a. 1. (When an element is in a condition in which it does not yet produce its function, it is called future; when it produces it, it is called present; when, having produced it, it ceases to work, it is past, its substance remaining the same.) Yaçom. Just as in an abacus the same ball receives different significations according to the place it is thrown in. If it is thrown in the place for units it means one, if in the place for hundreds it means a hundred, if in the place for thousands it means one thousand.

[1] Or, if *rūpa* stands for *svarūpa*, "its essence."

281, a. 3. (4) An advocate of contingency (*apekṣā*) is the venerable Buddhadeva. He is known to have maintained the principle that an element in the course of time receives this or that denomination on account of its relation to the former and the Yaçom. next moment. (An element is future with respect to the former one, be it past or present, it is present with respect to a former, i.e. past one or with respect to the next one, i.e. future one, it is past with respect to the next one, be it present or future.) Just as the same female may be called a mother (with respect to her children) and a daughter (with respect to her own mother).

Thus it is that all these four (lines of thought) are so many varieties of the theory which maintains Universal Existence. As regards the first of them, it is nothing else than the doctrine of the changing manifestations (of one eternal matter). Therefore it must be included in the Sānkhya system (which has already been rejected). As to the second, it is a confusion of all times, since it implies co-existence of all the aspects (of an element) at the same time. The passion of a man may be prominent towards one female, and merely existent (imperceptibly) towards another one, but what has this fact to do with the theory it is supposed to illustrate ? According to the fourth explanation, it would follow that all the three times are found together, included in one of them. Thus in the scope of the past time we can distinguish a former and a following moment. They will represent a past and a future time. Between them the inter-
281, a. 7. mediate moment will correspond to a present time. Thus it is that among all proposed explanations the (remaining one alone), the third in number, is right, that which maintains a change of condition (or function). According thereto the difference in time reposes on the difference in function: at the time when an element does not yet actually perform its function it is future; when performing it, it becomes present; when, after having performed it, it stops, it becomes past.

281, b. 1. *Sautrāntika.*—Although I perfectly understand all this, I do not see my way to admit that it implies a real existence of the past and of the future. For, if the past is really existent and the future likewise, what induces us (to make a distinction between them and) to call them past and future ?

Vaibhāṣika.—But have we not already explained it : the time of an element is settled in accordance with the time of its function.

Sautrāntika.—If this be the case, an eye which does not look at the present moment will not be present, because it does not perform its function ?

Vaibhāṣika.—It is present (because it performs its other functions) : it is the immediate cause (of the next moment of its existence and the remote cause) determining (its future character).

(Although an eye that does not look is not performing its function, it, nevertheless, is efficient in immediately producing and forecasting the homogeneousness of its future with its past and in producing its, so-called, co-operative result.[1] In that sense it is present.) Mchims-pa, ii, 166, a. 4.

Sautrāntika.—In that case the past will be the same as the present, since the past likewise produces such results—the past viewed as a cause of homogeneousness in consecutive moments,[2] as a general moral cause,[3] and as a cause requiring retribution [4]—all these causes would be present since they may perform their actual functions at the present moment.

Vaibhāṣika.—I call present a cause which exhibits at the present moment a double function—that of giving an immediate result

[1] The Sarvāstivādins establish several kinds of causal relations between the elements. If e.g. a moment of the sense of vision produces in the next moment a visual sensation, it is termed *kāraṇa-hetu* and its result *adhipati-phala*. This relation will be absent in the case of an inefficient condition of the organ of vision. But there are other relations between the moments of this organ. When the next moment is just the same as the foregoing one, thus evoking in the observer the idea of duration, this relation is termed *sabhāga-hetu* as to a *niṣyanda-phala*. If this moment appears in a stream (*santāna*) which is defiled by the presence of passions (*kleça*), this defiling character is inherited by the next moments, if no stopping of it is produced. Such a relation is called *sarvatraga-hetu* as to *niṣyanda-phala*. Finally every moment in a stream is under the influence of former deeds (*karma*) and may, in its turn, have an influence on future events. This relation is termed *vipāka-hetu* as to *vipāka-phala*. The simultaneity of the inseparable elements of matter will produce a co-operative result (*puruṣakāra-phala*). These last three relations must be existent even in the case of a non-operative moment of the sense of vision. Cf. *Ab. K.*, ii, 50 ff. ; O. Rosenberg, *Problems*, chap. xv.

[2] *Sabhāga-hetu.*

[3] *Sarvatraga-hetu.*

[4] *Vipāka-hetu.*

and that of determining the character of its remote future. A past cause, although it may produce a result at the present moment, does not, at present, determine its general character (which has been previously determined). Therefore the past is not the same as the present.

Sautrāntika.—If the time is settled according to efficiency, an element may be past inasmuch as its power of determining the general character of a remote result belongs to the past, and it may be present nevertheless, since it produces the result of the present moment. Thus a confusion of the characteristic signs of all the three times will arise, and I maintain that you are guilty
31, b. 3. of such confusion. Your standpoint leads to the absurdity of assuming actual or semi-actual past causes (i.e. semi-present elements), since the cause of homogeneousness and other past causes may produce a (present) result. A confusion of the essential natures of the three times is the consequence.

1, b. 4. (Part II.—*The case against Everlasting Elements*)

ārikā, v. 25. *Sautrāntika.*—To this we must make the following reply:—

What is it that keeps (an element from exhibiting its action)? And how is (the time of this action to be determined)? If it, the time of an element's existence, does not differ from the essence of the element itself, there will altogether be no time. If the element in the future and in the past exists just in the same sense as in the present, why is it future and past? The essence of the elements of existence (*dharmatā*) is deep!

1, b. 4. If the essence alone of the elements of existence persists throughout all the three times, but not their function, what is it that constitutes an impediment to this function? What is it that sometimes induces them to perform and sometimes keeps them back from performing their function?

Vaibhāṣika.—The function is performed when all the necessary conditions are present.

Sautrāntika.—This won't do! because (according to your theory) these conditions are always present. Again, as to the functions themselves, they likewise may be past, future, and present. They then require an explanation in their turn.

281, b. 6. Will you admit the existence of a second function (which will determine the time of the first)? or will you suppose that it neither is past, nor future, nor present, but that it, nevertheless, does exist? In this case this function will not be subject to the elementary forces of life (*saṃskṛta*) and will represent an immovable eternal entity (*asaṃskṛta*). For this reason you cannot maintain that, as long as an element does not yet perform its function, it is future.

Vaibhāṣika.—If the function of an element were something different from the element itself, your objections would be right. But since it is not different, they do not hold good. 281, b. 7.

Sautrāntika.—Then there is no time at all! If the function is the same as the substance, the elements will always remain identical. For what reason are they sometimes called past, sometimes future, and sometimes present?

Vaibhāṣika.—An element that has not yet appeared is future, one which has appeared and not yet disappeared is present, one which has disappeared is past. What is it you find unfounded in this explanation?

Sautrāntika.—The following point needs here to be established:—if the past and the future exist in the same sense as the present, as realities, why is it, then, that, being existent in the same sense, they are future and past? If the substance of the same element is alone (permanently) existent, what is the reason that it is spoken of as "having not yet appeared" or "gone"? What is it that does not appear later on and whose absence makes us call it "past"?

Thus it is that the notion of three times will altogether have no real foundation, as long as you don't accept the view that the elements appear into life out of non-existence and return again into non-existence after having been existing. (Your theory implies eternal existence of the elements.)

Vaibhāṣika.—It is absurd to maintain that it implies eternal existence! There are the four forces (of origination, decay, maintenance, and destruction) to which every element is subject, and the combination (of the permanent essence of an element with these forces produces its impermanent manifestations in life).

Sautrāntika.—Mere words! They cannot explain the origination and decay (which are going on in the process of life). An element, according to this view, is permanent and impermanent at the same time. This, indeed, is something quite new! It has been said on this occasion :—

a. 7. Maintained eternal essence;
Denied eternal being!
And yet no difference between
This essence and this being.
'Tis clearly a caprice
Of the Almighty!
'Tis spoken by His order!

(*Vaibhāṣika.*—But Buddha has said that there "is" a past and there "is" a future.)

Sautrāntika.—We, likewise, maintain that there "is" a past and there "is" a future. But this means that what has been formerly "is" past, and what, in the (presence of its causes), will happen "is" future. They exist in this sense only, not in reality.

b. 1. *Vaibhāṣika.*—Who has ever maintained that they exist just in the same sense in which the present exists?

Sautrāntika.—How can one exist otherwise?

Vaibhāṣika.—The essence of the past and of the future is (always) existent.

Sautrāntika.—If they are always existent, how is the (remarkable result) brought about that they are called past or future? Therefore the words of our Sublime Lord, "there *is* a past, there *is* a future," must be understood in another sense. He proffered them when discussing with the Ājīvikas (who denied moral responsibility for past deeds). He strongly opposed their doctrine, which denied the connexion between a past cause and a future result. In order to make it known that a former cause and a future result are something which happened formerly and will happen in future, he categorically declared: "There *is* a past, there *is* a future." For the word "is" acts as a particle (which may refer to something existent and to non-existence as well). As e.g. people will say: "there *is* absence of light" (before it has been kindled), "there *is* absence of light after (it has been put out)," or the "light *is* put out, but I did not put it out". When Buddha declared that there "is" a past and there "is" a future, he used the word "is" in that sense.

Had it been otherwise, it would be absolutely impossible to account for (the notions of) a past and a future.

Vaibhāṣika.—But, then, how are we to understand the words of our Sublime Lord when addressing the Lāguḍaçikhīyaka wandering ascetics (the bearers of a tress on the head and a stick in the hand)? Why did he declare: "a deed (which requires immediate retribution) is past, is accomplished, is finished, is gone, has disappeared, but, nevertheless, it does exist." What did these ascetics really deny? Not that the accomplished deed was past, (but that it could have some actual existence, i.e. some efficiency. Hence the words of Buddha imply an actual existence of the past). 282, b. 5.

Sautrāntika.—(No!) He meant that a force to produce retribution is driven by a past deed into the run (of combined elements which constitute an individual). Were it existent in reality, it would not be past. This is the only way in which this passage needs be understood, because on another occasion, in the sermon about "Non-substantiality as the Ultimate Truth",[1] the Sublime Lord has spoken thus: "when the organ of vision appears into life, there is absolutely nothing from which it proceeds, and when it vanishes, nought there is to which it retires. Therefore, O Brethren, this organ of vision has no former existence. Then it appears, and after having been existent it vanishes again." If a future organ of vision were existent, Buddha would never have declared that it appeared out of non-existence (out of nothing). 282, b. 7.

Vaibhāṣika.—(This passage means that), as far as the present time is concerned, it did not exist, and then appeared (in the scope of this time). 283, a. 2.

Sautrāntika.—Impossible! Time is not something different from the object (existing in it).

Vaibhāṣika.—But may not its essence have not been present and then have appeared?

Sautrāntika.—This would only prove that it had no (real) future existence.

(*The second argument of the Sarvāstivādins refuted*)

Sautrāntika.—Now your second argument is drawn from the circumstance that cognition, when arising, reposes on two factors: 283, a. 3.

[1] *Paramārtha-çūnyatā-sūtra*, Saṃyuktāgama, xiii, 22 (McGovern).

a perceptive faculty and a corresponding object. Here we must at first (consider the instance) of mental cognition reposing on the operation of the intellect and on a mental (not sensuous) object.[1] Is this object a real cause in the same sense as the intellect ? or is it a mere (passive) object realized by the intellect ? If it were a real active cause, how could events which must happen after the lapse of a thousand æons, or those which never will happen, possibly constitute an active cause of the corresponding cognition ? And the Final Deliverance, which is synonymous with the total cessation of every operation of all the elements of existence, how can it constitute a really active cause of its own conception ? But if, on the other hand, such objects are mere passive objects of the operating mind, then I maintain that they may be future and may be past.

a. 7. *Vaibhāṣika.*—If they altogether do not exist, how can they possibly be objects ?

Sautrāntika.—Their existence I admit, (understanding by existence) that very form in which they are conceived by us at the present moment in the present place.

a. 8. *Vaibhāṣika.*—And how are they conceived ?

Sautrāntika.—As past and as future. If somebody remembers a past object or a former feeling, he has never been observed to say " it exists ", but only " it did exist ".

(*The third argument of the Sarvāstivādins examined*)

b. 1. *Sautrāntika.*—As (to the cognition of past and future) sense objects, the past ones are remembered in that very form in which they were experienced when they were present, and the future ones are known to Buddhas just in that form in which they will appear at the time when they will be present.

Vaibhāṣika.—And if it be just the same existence (as the present one) ?

Sautrāntika.—Then it is present.

Vaibhāṣika.—If not ?

Sautrāntika.—(It is absent : and thus) it is proved that absence can be cognized just as well (as presence).

Vaibhāṣika.—But (will you not admit that the past and the future) are fragments of the present itself ?

[1] *dharmāḥ,* i.e. 64 *dharmas, āyatana* No. 12.

Sautrāntika.—No, because we are not conscious of apprehending fragments.

Vaibhāṣika.—But, then, it may represent the same stuff, with the mere (difference that in the past and the future) its atoms may be disjoined ?

Sautrāntika.—In that case, atoms will be eternally existent, and (all the process of life) will consist in their either combining or disjoining. There will altogether be no new origination, no real extinction, and thus you will become guilty of adhering to the (heretical) doctrine of the Ājīvikas.

Moreover, you will be contradicted by the scriptural passage 283, b. 4. (referred to above): "when the organ of vision is produced, it does not come from some other place; when it disappears, it is not going to be stored up in another place, etc."

On the other hand, it is impossible that feelings and other (mental phenomena), which have no atomic structure, should be divided into fragments. If remembered, they likewise are remembered in that very form in which they did appear and were experienced. And, if you suppose that they continue to exist in the same form, they must be eternal. If they do not, it will be proved that (a non-existent feeling) may be apprehended (by memory) just as well (as an existent one is apprehended by self-perception).

Vaibhāṣika.—If non-existence is capable of being apprehended, 283, b. 6. you must add to (the list of all things cognizable, i.e.) to the twelve bases of cognition (*āyatana*), a new category, the thirteenth, non-existence.

Sautrāntika.—Supposing I think about the absence of a thirteenth category, what will be then the object corresponding to my thought ?

Vaibhāṣika.—It will be this very (category, i.e. its) name.

Sautrāntika.—And what is it (generally speaking) that we apprehend, when we are expecting to hear a word which as yet is not pronounced ?

Vaibhāṣika.—It is nothing else than this very word.

Sautrāntika.—Then a person who desires not to hear this word, will be obliged to pronounce it!

Vaibhāṣika.—It may be the future condition of this word ?

Sautrāntika.—If it is something existent, why does it produce an idea of absence ?

Vaibhāṣika.—Then it may be its present absence ?

Sautrāntika.—No ! it is the same. (If this present absence is something existent, why does it produce an idea of non-existence?)

Vaibhāṣika.—Then it may be the characteristic sign of a future ; (this sign is absent at present, and gives rise to the idea of non-existence).

Sautrāntika.—This sign consists (in the fact that the future) will appear into existence out of a previous non-existence. Thus it is that both existence and non-existence may be objects of cognition.

84, a. 2. *Vaibhāṣika.*—And how do you explain the words of the future Buddha, who has spoken thus : " that these persons know or perceive things which do not exist in the world—this is impossible ! " ?

Sautrāntika.—These words (do not mean that non-existence cannot be an object of cognition, but they) have the following meaning :—" there are other, manifestly deluded, persons (who have not yet attained the divine power of vision : they) perceive things that never did exist. I perceive only existing (remote) things." If, on the contrary, every possible thought had only existing things for its object, what reason could there have been for doubting (the accuracy of the assertion of such people about what they were perceiving by their power of divine vision) ? or what would have been the difference (between the *bodhisattva's* real power of vision and the incomplete power of these men) ?
84, a. 5. It is inevitable that we should understand the passage in this sense, because it is confirmed by another scriptural passage, which begins with the words : " come unto me, ye monks, my pupils ! " and goes on until the following words are spoken : " what I am telling him in the morning becomes clearer at night, what I am conversing about at night becomes clearer to him next morning. He will cognize the existence of what does exist, the non-existence of what does not exist. Where something still higher exists, he will know that there is something still higher ; and where nothing higher exists, he will know that (it is the Final Deliverance, that) there is nothing higher than that ! " Therefore the argument (in favour of a real existence of the past,

that you have drawn from the supposed fact that) our intellect can have only existent things for its object—this argument is wrong.

(The fourth argument of the Sarvāstivādins examined)

Sautrāntika.—As to your next argument (in favour of the real existence of the past, viz. because it has a real) result—we must observe that we, the Sautrāntikas, never did maintain that a result can be produced from a past deed (directly). 284, a. 7.

Vaibhāṣika.—How is it produced, then ?

Sautrāntika.—(This deed) is the beginning of a peculiar chain of events (in the course of which the result appears sooner or later). A more detailed explanation of this point will be given later on, when we will refute the theory (of the Vātsīputrīyas, who) maintain the existence of an individual.[1] (As to your view, it is manifestly inconsistent.) What result can a past deed produce according to this view ? If the past and the future are actually existent, the result will necessarily be pre-existent from all eternity.

Vaibhāṣika.—(But we assume the existence of the force of generation ?)

Sautrāntika.—Well, then, it will be established that this force itself appears after having previously been non-existent ! In fact, if everything without any exception is pre-existent, there can be nothing that could have a force to produce anything ! In the end it comes to the same as the theory of the followers of Varṣagaṇya. According to them there is neither production of something new nor extinction of something existent: what exists is always existent, what does not exist will never become existent. 284, b. 1.

Vaibhāṣika.—But the force (of a past deed) may consist in " making present " (some already existing element) ?

Sautrāntika.—How is this " making present " to be understood? 284, b. 3

Vaibhāṣika.—It consists in removing (the result from one) place to another.

Sautrāntika.—Then the result would be eternally pre-existent. And, as to non-existent elements, how can they (be made to change place) ? Moreover, such " removing " means production (of a motion, i.e. of something) which previously did not exist.

[1] *Ab. K.*, ix, translated in my *Soul Theory*.

284, b. 5. *Vaibhāṣika.*—It may consist in a "specification" of the (everlasting) essence of an element?

Sautrāntika.—This, again, would prove that there is production of what previously did not exist. To conclude: the principle of Universal Existence, as far as exegetical literature is concerned, where it implies an actual existence of the past and of the future, does not hold good. On the contrary, it is all right if we strictly conform to the words of Scripture, where it is declared that "everything exists".

Vaibhāṣika.—And in what sense has it been declared in Scripture that "everything exists"?

Sautrāntika.—O Brahmins! it has been declared, "everything exists": that means no more than "the elements included in the twelve categories (*āyatana*) are existent".

Vaibhāṣika.—And the three times (are they not included among these elements)?

Sautrāntika.—(No, they are not!). How their existence is to be understood we have already explained.

(*The Sarvāstivādin reverts to his first argument*)

284, b. 7. *Vaibhāṣika.*—If the past and the future did not exist, how could it be possible that a man should be attracted by (a past and future passion) to a (past or future object of enjoyment)?

Sautrāntika.—This becomes possible because past passions leave residues (or produce seeds), which are the causes of new passions; these seeds are existent (and the saint has the capacity of keeping them down, of being independent of them). Therefore, a man can be bound by (past accesses of) passion. And it is in this sense that he can be allured by (future or past) objects, because the seeds of these passions, which are directed towards (past and future enjoyments), are always present in him.

Conclusion

Cf. Mchims-pa, ii, 167, b. 7. *Vaibhāṣika* (does not feel discountenanced by this series of arguments, and says:) We Vaibhāṣikas, nevertheless, maintain
285, a. 1. that the past and the future certainly do exist. But (regarding the everlasting essence of the elements of existence, we confess) that this is something we do not succeed in explaining, their essence is deep (it is transcendental), since its existence cannot

be established by rational methods.[1] (And as to the use we make of the notion of time in common life, it is contradictory. We use) the expression: "what appears vanishes" (implying that the same element appears and disappears, e.g.) "some matter appears and disappears". But we, likewise, say "one thing appears, another disappears", implying that one element, the future one, enters into life, and another one (the present one), stops. We also speak of the appearing of time (itself "the time is come"), because the element which enters into life is included in the notion of time. And we speak about being born "from time", since the future includes many moments (and only one of them actually enters into life).

End of the Episodical Investigation

[1] The Peking and Narthang Bstan-ḥgyur read here *drañ-bar mi nus-so.* This may mean that the remark of the Vaibhāṣika applies to the elements of mind alone, i.e. the elements that cannot be carried from one place to another. But Saṅghabhadra's text points to a reading *bçad-par mi nus-so,* which undoubtedly is the correct one, since it is supported by the translation of Hiuen-Tsang. The corruption must be very old, since the block-print of the Aga monastery, which is founded on old sources coming from Derge, repeats it and it is retained by Mchims-pa.

APPENDIX II

TABLES OF THE ELEMENTS ACCORDING TO THE SARVĀSTIVĀDINS

General View

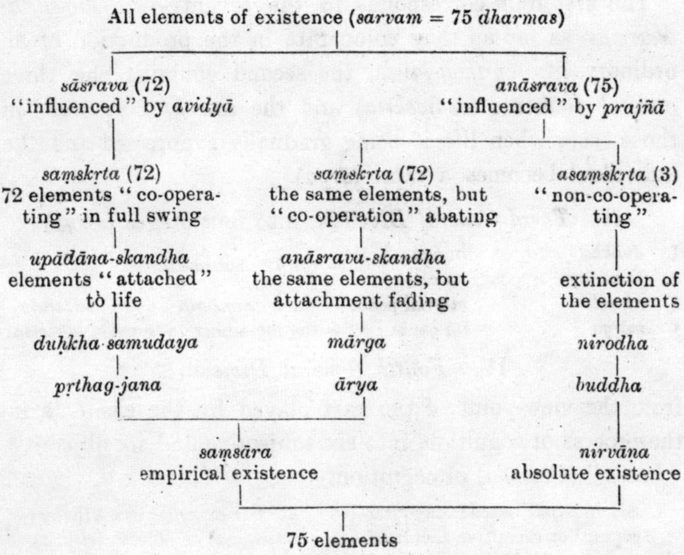
All elements of existence (*sarvam* = 75 *dharmas*)
sāsrava (72)
"influenced" by *avidyā*
anāsrava (75)
"influenced" by *prajñā*
saṃskṛta (72)
72 elements "co-operating" in full swing
saṃskṛta (72)
the same elements, but "co-operation" abating
asaṃskṛta (3)
"non-co-operating"
upādāna-skandha
elements "attached" to life
anāsrava-skandha
the same elements, but attachment fading
extinction of the elements
duḥkha samudaya
mārga
nirodha
pṛthag-jana
ārya
buddha
saṃsāra
empirical existence
nirvāṇa
absolute existence
75 elements

Classification of all Elements of Existence

(*Sarvam* = *anātman* = 12 *āyatanas* = 18 *dhātus* = 75 *dharmas*)

I. *First General Division*

1. ***saṃskṛta*** . . co-operating, impermanent . . 72 dharmas.
2. ***asaṃskṛta*** . . non-co-operating, immutable .. . 3 „

II. *Second General Division*

1. ***sāsrava*** . . "influenced" by passions, process of life in full swing.
2. ***anāsrava*** . . "uninfluenced" by passions, process of life abating and suppressed.

The first item corresponds to the seventy-two *saṃskṛta-dharmas* as far as they co-operate in the production of an ordinary life (*pṛthag-jana*), the second contains the three eternal elements (*asaṃskṛta*) and the *saṃskṛta* as well, in those cases when life is being gradually suppressed and the individual becomes a saint (*ārya*).

III. *Third General Division*, into four stages (*satya*)

1. ***duḥkha*** . .	unrest	= the 72 ***sāsrava-dharma***.	
2. ***samudaya*** . .	its cause		
3. ***nirodha*** . .	eternal peace	= the 3 ***asaṃskṛta***	***anāsrava-dharma***.
4. ***mārga*** . .	its cause	= the remaining ***anāsrava***	

IV. *Fourth General Division*

from the view-point of the part played by the elements in the process of cognition, into six subjective and six objective "bases" (*āyatana*) of cognition.

I. Six internal bases (*adhyātma-āyatana*) or receptive faculties (*indriya*).	II. Six external bases (*bāhya-āyatana*) or objects (*viṣaya*).
1. Sense of vision (*cakṣur-indriya-āyatana*).	7. Colour and shape (*rūpa-āyatana*).
2. Sense of audition (*çrotra-indriya-āyatana*).	8. Sound (*çabda-āyatana*).
3. Sense of smelling (*ghrāṇa-indriya-āyatana*).	9. Odour (*gandha-āyatana*).
4. Sense of taste (*jihvā-indriya-āyatana*).	10. Taste (*rasa-āyatana*).
5. Sense of touch (*kāya-indriya-āyatana*).	11. Tangibles (*spraṣṭavya-āyatana*).
6. Faculty of the intellect or consciousness (*mana-indriya-āyatana*).	12. Non-sensuous objects (*dharma-āyatana* or *dharmāḥ*).

In this classification the eleven first items correspond to eleven elements (*dharma*), each including one. The twelfth item contains all the remaining sixty-four elements, and it is therefore called *dharma-āyatana* or simply *dharmāḥ*, i.e. the *remaining* elements.

V. *Fifth General Division*

into eighteen classes (*dhātu* = *gotra*) of elements represented in the composition of an individual stream of life (*santāna*) in the different planes of existence.

I. Six *indriyas*.			II. Six *viṣayas*.
1.	*cakṣur-dhātu*, sense of vision.	7.	*rūpa-dhātu*, colour.
2.	*çrotra-dhātu*, ,, audition.	8.	*çabda-dhātu*, sound.
3.	*ghrāṇa-dhātu*, ,, smelling.	9.	*gandha-dhātu*, odour.
4.	*jihvā-dhātu*, ,, taste.	10.	*rasa-dhātu*, taste.
5.	*kāya-dhātu*, ,, touch.	11.	*spraṣṭavya-dhātu*, tangibles.
6.	*mano-dhātu*, ,, faculty of intellect.	12.	*dharma-dhātu*, or *dharmāḥ*, non-sensuous objects.

III. Six *vijñānas*.

13.	Visual consciousness		(*cakṣur-vijñāna-dhātu*).
14.	Auditory	,,	(*çrotra-vijñāna-dhātu*).
15.	Olfactory	,,	(*ghrāṇa-vijñāna-dhātu*).
16.	Gustatory	,,	(*jihvā-vijñāna-dhātu*).
17.	Tactile	,,	(*kāya-vijñāna-dhātu*).
18.	Non-sensuous	,,	(*mano-vijñāna-dhātu*).

Ten of these *dhātus* contain one *dharma* each (Nos. 1–5 and 6–11); the *dhātu* No. 12 contains sixty-four *dharmas* (forty-six *caitta*, fourteen *citta-viprayukta*, three *asaṃskṛta*, and *avijñapti*); consciousness, representing a single *dharma*, is split into seven *dhātus*, No. 6 and Nos. 13–18.

On the sensuous plane of existence (*kāma-Dhātu*) the individual streams (*santāna*) are composed of all the eighteen *dhātus*. In the world of "Reduced Matter" (*rūpa-Dhātu*) the *dhātus* Nos. 9–10 and 15–16 are absent, and the individuals are composed of only fourteen *dhātus*. In the Immaterial Worlds (*arūpa-Dhātu*) they are composed of only three *dhātus*, Nos. 6, 12, and 18, since all matter and sensuous consciousness does not exist there.

The six *viṣayas* are *viṣaya* in regard to the six *indriyas*, but *ālambana* in regard to the six *vijñānas*.

VI. *Sixth division*, of the seventy-two active elements (*saṃskṛta-dharma*) into five groups (*skandha*).

1.	*rūpa-skandha* .	the physical elements, matter .	11	dharmas.
2.	*vedanā-skandha* .	feeling	1	,,
3.	*sanjñā-skandha* .	conception	1	,,
4.	*saṃskāra-skandha*.	will and other forces . . .	58	,,
5.	*vijñāna-skandha* .	pure consciousness (without content)	1	,,
		Together . .	72	,,

Group means collection, viz. of *dharmas* past, present, and future, remote and near, pure and defiled, etc. The *asaṃskṛta* are not included in this division, but the other *anāsrava*, as well as the *sāsrava*, are included. When the *sāsrava* alone are meant, the groups are called *upādāna-skandha*, i.e. elements of "attachment" to life. Other synonyms are *raṇa* "struggle", *duḥkha* "unrest", *duḥkha-samudaya* "cause of unrest", *loka* "mundane existence", *dṛṣṭi-sthiti* "the place where the belief in the existence of personality obtains", *bhava* "existence" simply, since by existence simply the usual existence of ordinary men is meant.

When the *skandhas* embrace all the *saṃskṛta-dharmas*, the *sāsrava* and *anāsrava* as well, they receive, in contradistinction to the *upādāna-skandhas*, other names: *adhvānaḥ* "the (three) times", *kathā-vastu* "objects of speech", *saniḥsaraṇa* "elements to be suppressed", *savastuka* "having empirical reality", or "being subject to causality". The *skandha* No. 4 contains all the *caitta-dharmas*, except *vedanā* and *sanjñā*, i.e. forty-four mental faculties with *cetanā*, the will as the principal one, and fourteen general forces (*citta-viprayukta*).

The Single Elements of Matter (rūpa), Mind (citta-caitta), Forces (viprayukta-saṃskāra), and Eternity (asaṃskṛta)

A. Matter (rūpa)

1. *cakṣur-indriya*, translucent matter (*rūpa-prasāda*) conveying visual sensations.
2. *çrotra-indriya*, translucent matter (*rūpa-prasāda*) conveying auditory sensations.

3. *ghrāṇa-indriya*, translucent matter (*rūpa-prasāda*) conveying olfactory sensations.
4. *jihvā-indriya*, translucent matter (*rūpa-prasāda*) conveying taste sensations.
5. *kāya-indriya*, translucent matter (*rūpa-prasāda*) conveying tactile sensations.
6. *rūpa-viṣaya*, visual sense-data.
7. *çabda-viṣaya*, auditory „
8. *gandha-viṣaya*, olfactory „
9. *rasa-viṣaya*, taste „
10. *spraṣṭavya-viṣaya*, tactile „
11. *avijñapti*, unmanifested matter, the vehicle of moral qualities.

Matter is divided into primary (*bhūta* = *mahābhūta*) and secondary (*bhautika*). Four atoms of primary matter, one from each *mahābhūta*, are necessary to support one *bhautika*-atom. Only No. 10, the tactile class, contains both all the primary and some secondary kinds of tactibility: all the other classes contain only secondary, supported, kind of matter.

The Four Universal Elements of Matter (*mahābhūta*)

1. *pṛthivī*, element manifesting itself as hard-stuff, or repulsion.
2. *ap*, „ „ „ viscous-stuff, or attraction.
3. *tejas*, „ „ „ heat-stuff.
4. *īraṇa*, „ „ „ motion-stuff.

Avijñapti is a variety of *karma*. Actions can be either mental (*cetanā*) or physical—corporeal and vocal acts (*kāyika*- and *vācika-karma*). They are also divided into manifest acts (*vijñapti*) and unmanifested ones—*avijñapti*. The latter are, for our habits of thought, not acts, but their results, they are not physical, but moral. If a novice has taken the vows he has committed a physical, vocal action, which is *vijñapti*, but the lasting result is some moral excellence hidden in consciousness, and this is *avijñapti*. It constitutes a link between the act and its future retribution; it is, therefore, the same as *saṃskāra*, *apūrva*, *adṛṣṭa* of the Brahmanical systems. Although by no means physical, since it lacks the general characteristic of matter which is impenetrability (*sapratighatva*), it nevertheless is brought by the Sarvāstivādins (not by others) under the head of *rūpa*, because of its close connexion with the physical act upon which it follows as a shadow cast from an object always follows that object.

B. Consciousness, Pure, without Content (citta = manas = vijñāna)

1. *manas*, consciousness in the rôle of an independent, sixth, perceptive faculty, cognizing the non-sensuous, or abstract, objects (*dharmāḥ*): it represents the preceding moment with regard to the *mano-vijñāna*.
2. *cakṣur-vijñāna*, the same pure consciousness when associated with the visual sense.
3. *çrotra-vijñāna*, the same pure consciousness when associated with the auditory sense.
4. *ghrāṇa-vijñāna*, the same pure consciousness when associated with the olfactory sense.
5. *jihvā-vijñāna*, the same pure consciousness when associated with the taste sense.
6. *kāya-vijñāna*, the same pure consciousness when associated with the tactile sense.
7. *mano-vijñāna*, the same pure consciousness when associated with a previous moment of the same run of consciousness without participation of any of the five senses.

C. The forty-six Mental Elements (caitta-dharma) or Faculties intimately combining with the Element of Consciousness (citta-samprayukta-saṃskāra)

They are divided into—

1.	10	*citta-mahābhūmika-dharma*, Mental Faculties.	
2.	10	*kuçala-mahābhūmika-dharma*	Moral Forces.
3.	6	*kleça-mahābhūmika-dharma*	
4.	1	*akuçala-mahābhūmika-dharma*	
5.	10	*upakleça-(parītta-)bhūmika-dharma*	
6.	8	*aniyata-bhūmika-dharma*	
Together .	46		

a. *Ten General Mental Faculties present in every moment of Consciousness (citta-mahābhūmika)*—

1. *vedanā* . . faculty of feeling (pleasant, unpleasant, indifferent).
2. *sanjñā* . . „ concepts (capable of coalescing with a word).
3. *cetanā* . . „ will, conscious effort (*citta-abhisaṃskāra*, *citta-praspanda*).
4. *sparça* . . „ sensation (comparable to a first " contact between object, sense-organ, and consciousness).

5. *chanda* . . faculty of desire (*abhiprete vastuny abhilāṣa*).
6. *prajñā* (= *mati*) „ understanding, discriminating (*yena saṅkīrṇā iva dharmāḥ puṣpāṇīva pravicīyante*).
7. *smṛti* . . „ memory (*cetaso 'pramoṣaḥ*).
8. *manasikāra* . „ attention.
9. *adhimokṣa* . „ inclination (*ālambanasya guṇato 'vadhāraṇam*).
10. *samādhi* . „ concentration (*yena cittam prabandhena ekatrālambane vartate*).

b. Ten Universally "good" Moral Forces, present in every favourable moment of Consciousness (kuçala-mahā-bhūmika)—

1. *çraddhā* . faculty of belief in retribution, the purity of mind, the reverse of passion (*cittasya prasādaḥ*).
2. *vīrya* . . „ courage in good actions (*kuçala-kriyāyāṃ cetaso 'tyutsāhaḥ*).
3. *upekṣā* . . „ equanimity, indifference (*cittasya samatā, yad-yogāt cittam anābhogaṃ vartate*).
4. *hrī* . . „ shyness, modesty, humility, being ashamed with reference to oneself (*gauravam*). The reverse of IV, 1.
5. *apatrapā* . „ aversion to things objectionable, feeling disgust with reference to other peoples' objectionable actions (*avadye bhayadarçitā*). The reverse of IV, 2.
6. *alobha* . . „ absence of love.
7. *adveṣa* . . „ absence of hatred.
8. *ahiṃsā* . . „ causing no injury.
9. *pras*[*ç*]*rabdhi* „ mental dexterity (*cittasya karmaṇyatā, cittasya lāghavam*).
10. *apramāda* . „ acquiring and preserving good qualities (*kuçalānāṃ dharmāṇāṁ pratilambha-niṣevaṇam*).

c. Six Universally "Obscured" Elements present in every unfavourable moment of Consciousness (kleça-mahābhūmika)—

1. *moha* (= *avidyā*) faculty of ignorance, the reverse of *prajñā* (I, 6), and therefore the primordial cause of the commotion (*duḥkha*) of the world-process.
2. *pramāda* . „ carelessness, the reverse of *apramāda*, II, 10.
3. *kausīdya* . „ mental heaviness, clumsiness, the reverse of *prasrabdhi*, II, 9.
4. *açraddhā* „ disturbed mind, the reverse of *çraddhā*, II, 1.
5. *styāna* . . „ sloth, indolence, inactive temperament.

6. *auddhatya* .	faculty of	being addicted to pleasure and sports, sanguine temperament (*cetaso' nupaçamaḥ, nṛtya-gītādi-çṛṅgāra-veçyā-alaṃkāra-kāyaud-dhatya-sanniçraya-dāna-karmakaḥ caitasiko dharmaḥ*).

These six faculties are not always absolutely bad; they sometimes may be indifferent (*avyākṛta*) for the progress towards Final Deliverance, but they are nevertheless always "obscured" (*nivṛta* = *āchādita* = *kliṣṭa*) by promoting the belief in an existing personality (*satkāya-anugrāha-dṛsti-samprayukta*). Always bad (*akuçalāv eva*) are the following two—

d. Two Universally "bad" Elements present in every unfavourable moment of Consciousness (akuçala-mahā-bhūmika-dharma)—

1. *āhrīkya* .	faculty of	irreverence (*agauravaṃ* = *apratīçatā*,[1] *yad-yogād guṇeṣu guṇavatsu ca pudgaleṣu gauravaṃ na karoti*), arrogance, want of humility (*abhaya-vaça-vartitā*). The reverse of II, 4 (*gaurava-pratidvandvo dharmaḥ*).
2. *anapatrāpya* .	"	not feeling indignant at offences done by others (*avadye sadbhir garhite bhaya-a-darçitvam*). The reverse of II, 5.

e. Ten Vicious Elements of limited occurrence (upakleça-(parītta-)bhūmika-dharma)—

1. *krodha*	faculty of	anger, violence (*vyāpāda-vihiṃsā-varjitaḥ sattvāsattvayor āghātaḥ*).
2. *mrakṣa* . .	"	hypocrisy, deceit (of courtiers and others).
3. *mātsarya* .	"	envy.
4. *īrṣyā* . .	"	jealousy.
5. *pradāsa* .	"	approving objectionable things (*sāvadya-vastu-parāmarça*).
6. *vihiṃsā* .	"	causing harm, menacing.
7. *upanāha* .	"	breaking friendship.
8. *māyā* . .	"	deceit.
9. *çāṭya* . .	"	perfidy, trickery.
10. *mada* . .	"	complacency, self-admiration (cf. *māna*, VI, 7).

These ten elements are described as purely mental (*mano-bhūmikā eva*); they are never associated with any of the

[1] *pratīça* = *guru-sthānīya*.

five varieties of sensuous consciousness (*na panca-vijñāna-kāyikāḥ*), they cannot combine with the four alternating *kleças* (*rāga, dveṣa, māna, vicikitsā*), but with *moha* = *avidyā* alone, the purely mental *kleça*. They must be suppressed by knowledge (*dṛṣṭi-heya*), not by concentration (*bhāvanā-heya*). For all these reasons they are classified as vices of a limited scope (*parītta-bhūmika*).

f. *Eight Elements not having any definite place in the above system, but capable of entering into various combinations* (*aniyata-bhūmi-dharma*)—

1.	*kaukṛtya*	.	faculty of repenting.
2.	*middha* (= *nidrā*)	„	absent-mindedness, dreamy state of mind.
3.	*vitarka* . .	„	a searching state of mind.
4.	*vicāra* . .	„	a fixing state of mind.
5.	*rāga* . .	„	love, passion.
6.	*dveṣa* . .	„	hatred.
7.	*māna* . .	„	pride, an exagerated opinion of one's own pre-eminence by real or imagined qualifications (cf. *mada*, V, 10).
8.	*vicikitsā* .	„	a doubting turn of mind.

Kaukṛtya is brought under this head because it neither has a place among the universal faculties, nor has it a definitely "good" or definitely "bad" significance: it can mean repentance for a bad deed and being sorry for having e.g. overdone in charity.

Middha can also have various moral aspects.

Vitarka and *vicāra* are universal only in the *kāma-Dhātu*.

Rāga, *dveṣa*, *māna*, and *vicikitsā* are four *kleças*, the fifth being *moha* placed in III, 1. *Moha* is a universal "defiler", entering in every unfavourable conscious moment, but the other four "defilers" cannot combine with one another; if there is *rāga* associated with one's consciousness, there can be no association with *dveṣa* at the same time. Thus it is that in every favourable, "good" moment, consciousness is associated with at least twenty-two elements: the ten universal ones (I, 1–10), the ten universally good ones, and *vitarka*, *vicāra* (VI, 4–5). If repentance (VI, 1) is added, the number will increase by one. In every unfavourable or "bad" moment the minimum number will be twenty elements: the ten universal ones (I, 1–10), the six universally "obscured" (III, 1–6), the two universally bad (IV, 1–2), and *vitarka, vicāra* (VI, 4–5). If all the *saṃskṛta-lakṣaṇas, citta* itself, its *lakṣaṇas* and *upalakṣaṇas* are taken into account, the number will increase accordingly (cf. p. 30, n. 2). Vasubandhu remarks that it is very difficult to distinguish all these elements even in the long run, let alone in a moment, but difficult does not mean impossible. Contradictory elements, as e.g. pleasure and pain, cannot enter into the same combination, but contradiction is often only on the surface, e.g. *styāna* and *auddhatya*, an inactive and an exuberant element, are present in every vicious moment, it is some indulging in vice and some active participation. Whether the individual or the conscious state shall be more passive or more active depends on the occasional predominance of one element over the others. In every moment, or mental state, there always is one predominant element, just as in material substances we have earth, water, fire, and air, according to the predominance of one of the *mahābhūtas* (cf. p. 13). Among the universally good elements indifference (*upekṣā*, II, 3) and inclination (*adhimokṣa*, II, 9) are not contradictory: they are directed towards different objects: indifference towards pain and pleasure, and inclination towards good deeds, they can go together. But *apramāda* (II, 10) and *pramāda* (III, 2) are the reverse of one another, not mutual absence alone, and therefore they never can combine.

Vitarka, Vicāra.

Vitarka and *vicāra* are sub-conscious operations of the mind (*na niçcaya-dharmau*). *Vitarka* is "an indistinct murmur of the mind" (*mano-jalpa*), which is searching (*paryeṣaka*) after its object. In its initial stage (*anatyūha-avasthāyām*) it is simply a move of will (*cetanā-viçeṣa*); when emerging into the conscious plane (*atyūha-avasthāyām*), it becomes a certain thought (*prajñā-viçeṣa*). *Vicāra* is also an "indistinct murmur of the mind", but it is attempting to fix (*pratyavekṣaka*) its object; it has the same two stages; it is also characterized as a refinement (*sūkṣmatā*) of the coarser (*audārika*) *vitarka*. Since both these functions are associated with sense-consciousness, they very nearly approach the Kantian doctrine of synthesis of apprehension preceded by the mind running through a variety of sense-impressions, as far as they are sub-conscious operations of the mind preceding a definite sense perception. The Vaibhāṣikas maintain that there is some *vitarka* (= *vikalpa*) in every moment of consciousness; they then call it *svabhāva-vikalpa*; but Vasubandhu seems to admit "pure sensation" (reine Sinnlichkeit) without any participation of discursive thought (*vikalpa*). Cf. *Ab. K.* i, 30; ii, 33. *Vyāsa-bhāṣya* in i, 44, according to Professor B. Seal (*Positive Sciences*, p. 18), trans. pure intuition (*nirvicāra-nirvikalpa-prajñā*) and "empirical" intuition (*savicāra-nirvikalpa-prajñā*); the latter contains the three relations of Space, Time, and Causation, in addition to pure consciousness.

D. Forces which can neither be included among Material nor among Spiritual Elements (rūpa-citta-viprayukta-saṃskāra)

1. *prāpti* . .	a force which controls the collection of the elements in an individual stream of life (*santāna*).
2. *aprāpti* .	a force which occasionally keeps some elements in abeyance in an individual *santāna*.
3. *nikāya-sabhāgatā*	a force producing generality or homogeneity of existences, the counterpart of the realistic generality of the Vaiçeṣikas.
4. *āsanjñika* .	a force which (automatically, as a result of former deeds,) transfers an individual into the realms of unconscious trance.
5. *asanjñi-samāpatti* .	a force stopping consciousness and producing the unconscious trance (through an effort).
6. *nirodha-samāpatti*	a force stopping consciousness and producing the highest, semi-conscious, dreamy trance.
7. *jīvita* . .	the force of life-duration, a force which at the time of birth forecasts the moment of death, just as the force with which an arrow is discharged forecasts the moment when it will fall down.

8.	*jāti*	origination	the four *saṃskṛta-lakṣaṇas*, cf. p. 39 above.
9.	*sthiti*	subsistence	
10.	*jarā*	decay	
11.	*anityatā*	extinction	
12.	*nāma-kāya*	the force imparting significance to words.	
13.	*pada-kāya*	the force imparting significance to sentences.	
14.	*vyanjana-kāya*	the force imparting significance to articulate sounds.	

E. Immutable Elements (asamskṛta-dharma)

1.	*ākāça*	space (empty).
2.	*pratisankhyā-nirodha*	the suppression of the manifestations of an element (*dharma*) through the action of understanding (*prajñā*), as e.g. after having realized that the existence of a personality is an illusion a kind of eternal blank is substituted for this wrong idea.
3.	*apratisankhyā-nirodha*	the same cessation produced not through knowledge, but in a natural way, through the extinction of the causes that produced a manifestation, as e.g. the extinction of the fire when there is no more fuel.

F. Causal Interconnexion of Elements (hetu-pratyaya)

4 Pratyaya.	6 Hetu.	5 Phala.
1. *hetu-pratyaya.*	1. *sahabhū-hetu.*	1. *puruṣakāra-phala.*
	2. *samprayukta-hetu.*	
	3. *sabhāga-hetu.*	2. *niṣyanda-phala.*
	4. *sarvatraga-hetu.*	
	5. *vipāka-hetu.*	3. *vipāka-phala.*
2. *samanantara-pratyaya.*		
3. *ālambana-pratyaya.*		
4. *adhipati-pratyaya.*	6. *kāraṇa-hetu.*	4. *adhipati-phala.*
		5. *visaṃyoga-phala.*

As to the meaning, cf. pp. 30 ff. *Samanantara-pratyaya* (= *upasarpaṇa-pratyaya*) is similar to the *samavāyi-kāraṇa* of the Vaiçeṣikas. *Ālambana*, cf. p. 59, n. 1. *Adhipati-pratyaya* and *kāraṇa-hetu* are similar to the *karaṇa* (= *sādhakatamaṃ kāraṇam*) of the Vaiçeṣikas. *Visaṃyoga-phala* is *nirvāṇa*.

G. The twelve consecutive stages in the ever-revolving Life-process

(*Āvasthika* or *prākarṣika pratītya-samutpāda*)

I. Former Life.

1.	*avidyā*	delusion (*caitta-dharma*, III, 1).
2.	*saṃskāra*	(= *karma*)

II. Present Life.

3. *vijñāna* . . .	first moment of a new life, the moment of conception (= *pratisandhi-vijñāna*).
4. *nāma-rūpa* . .	the five *skandhas* in the embryo before the formation of the sense-organs.
5. *ṣaḍ-āyatana* . .	the formation of the organs.
6. *sparça* . . .	organs and consciousness begin to co-operate.
7. *vedanā* . . .	definite sensations.
8. *tṛṣṇā* . . .	awakening of the sexual instinct, beginning of new *karma*.
9. *upādāna* . .	various pursuits in life.
10. *bhava* . . .	life, i.e. various conscious activities (= *karma-bhava*).

III. Future Life.

11. *jāti* . .	rebirth.
12. *jarā-maraṇa* . .	new life, decay, and death.

The five *skandhas* are present during the whole process ; the different stages receive their names from the predominant *dharma* (cf. p. 28, n. 3). The first two stages indicate the origin of the life-process (*duḥkha-samudaya*).

In regard to a future life Nos. 8–10 perform the same function as Nos. 1–2 in regard to the present life. Therefore the series represents an ever revolving "wheel".

INDEX

I. PROPER NAMES

II. SANSCRIT TERMS